The
Discipleship
Lifestyle

How disciples develop disciples

Gary Gibbs

DEDICATION

No human has shaped me, adjusted me, challenged me
more than Sally Gibbs.

No human has loved me more than she has.

Now in our fifth decade of marriage, there is no one
I would rather 'do life' with.

I still love you. I always will!

THANK YOU!

There is the inevitable danger that when an author includes a list of people to whom he owes a debt of gratitude, it could end up doubling the amount of pages in the book! I did want to show my appreciation to a small bunch who have helped bring 'The Discipleship Lifestyle' into being.

Way back in the 1980s, Mark Mumford produced some very helpful seminars and notes on the meaning of discipleship. Recently, Mark was kind enough to dig those notes out and send them to me: some of what follows in the book found its beginnings way back in those heady days! We were colleagues in ministry for around a quarter of a century and those years significantly moulded and shaped me.

I am grateful to my current boss, Chris Cartwright, General Superintendent of the Elim Pentecostal Churches and my fellow Heads of Ministry, Iain Hesketh and Dave Newton for encouragement and suggestions on improving the content. Its great serving with you guys!

Keith and Judy Warrington offered love, wisdom and knowledge in equal measures. Amazing!

Mark Greenwood is one of the finest and most gifted evangelists in the United Kingdom. I'm so glad to count him as a close friend. Without him pushing me and generously providing all kinds of practical help, the book would still be a Word document sitting on my laptop. He even designed the cover! Thanks mate!

Finally, I have found the folks at Verité CM Ltd to be not only efficient business people, but also real Christians! Chris, Karen and the rest of your gang, you're a credit to the printing and publishing world!

FOREWORD

The pile of 'to read' books in my study is massive. In fact I could probably make it even higher without much trying. Why? Because there are a lots of good books out there on so many subjects that I would like to, and need to, boost my knowledge and increase my practice.

Making disciples is the priority of any Christian and as such any book on this subject should be at the top of the pile if not already open in our hands being read and actioned.

When Gary asked me to write the foreword I was deeply honoured because I have a huge amount of respect and love for him. This is a man who has seen thousands upon thousands of people give their lives to Christ and they continue to follow him today. I literally meet people on a regular basis whose story of conversion features Gary very significantly. Furthermore, Gary has stayed passionate about those who don't know Jesus as well as faithful to and in love with the Jesus he wants them to know.

As well as his years of faithful service as an evangelist, Gary has gathered a breadth and depth of knowledge about biblical evangelism. Coupled with a great ability to communicate as a speaker and writer, Gary is a treasure chest of resource honed in the rigours of local church life.

It is true that you can do evangelism without making disciples but you can't make disciples without doing evangelism and so this book, written by an evangelist who is interested in disciples and not just decisions is a real gift to the church. It's a fusion of food for thought and practical help so that making disciples can become your default setting as well as something you enjoy.

I really like the way Gary has made this book into bite-size chunks but also gives space to think and reflect about what you have read. Sure, you can race through this 'holiday read' style but I would encourage you to take advantage of the thoughtful way Gary has chosen to deliver the content. Go on a devotional journey to become a better disciple which will enable you to take others on the same journey - there is no greater privilege and no better way to live life for God.

Mark Greenwood

CONTENTS

DISCIPLESHIP:

Introduction

If you are anything like me, when I pick up a book and consider whether I'm going to spend my hard-earned cash on it and also whether I will even bother to read it, there is a basic question or two in my mind:

"Is this writer aiming at me? And do I need to learn what he/she is writing about?"

The answers to both questions are simple: if you are following Jesus, whether that's been for one day or for multiple decades, I wrote this for you. And discipleship lies at the very centre of what it means to be an authentic Christian.

My contention is that every one of us is ideally called to a life of discipleship both in terms of being trained and equipped ourselves but also by investing what God has deposited in us into the lives of others. For this reason you'll discover that sometimes, even within the same chapter, we jump around a little! I'll be describing what it means to lead someone in the way of Jesus and then the text will be about the one being led. I want you to see the two sides of the coin because a church-based discipleship culture depends upon us all being and doing both ends of this.

So here's how it all began for me...

Tom Hall was 99 years old when he left this planet in the Spring of 2020. He had followed Jesus since the age of 14. As an apprentice coal mine engineer in County Durham, he was lying in a narrow coal seam with an 18 year old believer who took an opportunity to share his faith. Right there and then, Tom said a 'Big Yes' to Jesus and surrendered his life to the Lord.

Fast forward forty years and the now Reverend Thomas Hall shared the Good News with me, an irreligious sixth form student who up until that point had been trying to find meaning, satisfaction and fulfilment through sport, alcohol and the opposite sex. It was a Monday afternoon in May 1974 at around 2pm when the love and forgiveness of God seemed to flood through me. What a blast!

Tom became a spiritual dad to me during those first few years. As an insensitive teenager, I would often keep him up into the early hours of the morning asking him all sorts of questions about scripture, lifestyle, future direction, etc. He gave me some great counsel, but more than that, he was the real deal in the way he lived his life.

I don't think Tom would ever have thought that he was disciple making – we didn't really use that language much in the mid-1970s – but that's what was happening.

At the time of writing, I've been following Jesus for 47 years and, on reflection, I'm aware of a number of people who have enabled me to grow as a believer. Most readers would not recognise the names of Dave Coles, Ken McGreavy, Chris Warwick, Mark Mumford, Mark Ryan, Jason Heron and Dave Ayling. There have been numerous other friends who have sharpened me through the years, but whether in a formal way or a more nuanced manner, I am grateful to God for all of those who have influenced me and enabled me to walk with Jesus.

I have no doubt however that the human who has shaped, challenged, taught and encouraged me more than anyone else over more than four decades (and counting) is Mrs Sally Gibbs. My wife is a straight-talking Yorkshire woman who doesn't carry hidden agendas. She is highly intelligent, extremely attractive and fiercely loyal. I'm so glad she agreed to marry me when I phoned her in the early hours of January 1st 1979 (don't ask!).

When I die I will be cremated. But if I was to be buried, my greatest fear would be to have an inscription on my tombstone which read 'He Had Potential'. I believe that any attempt at independent Christian living is a contradiction in terms: we were created, and recreated for relationships which shape us and make us.

The usefulness of this book will not be in giving you lots of knowledge, although I trust that the content will not be overly simplistic. My hope is that having read it you will do something! That you will pursue godly input into your life based on accountable relationships and that you will also look for divinely engineered opportunities to equip others.

In the early days of Methodism, a 'serious man' challenged John Wesley with these words

> *"Sir, you wish to serve God and go to heaven?*
> *Remember that you cannot serve him alone. You*
> *therefore must find companions or make them. The Bible*
> *knows nothing of solitary religion."*

Wesley must have taken this very much to heart as he formed new believers into 'classes' or small groups where through challenge, encouragement and openness, disciples of Jesus were developed.

We are born again not to live as hermits, isolated from everyone except God. We are part of a family and offered the privilege of a shared life both with Him and with our brothers and sisters in Christ. It's actually in this dynamic of a vertical relationship with the Lord and horizontal, deep friendship with other Christians that we experience authentic transformation.

The end goal as I think you'll see, is that we become more and more shaped into the image of the One who invites us to follow Him!

Gary Gibbs, Malvern, August 2021

DISCIPLESHIP: WHAT'S IN A WORD?
Setting the Scene/Defining the Theme

'Triskaidekaphobia' is a long word. What does it mean? If you are a quiz addict, a genius or simply lucky (!!), you may well know the answer. It's having an extreme fear of the number thirteen. Of course, you shouldn't use the word in normal conversation unless you are clear about its meaning and it fits the context of the chat!

'Discipleship' is not quite as long, but what does it mean? In recent years it has become a 'buzz word' in the Christian world. The challenge we face is that it is understood differently in various Church tribes and therefore we are not quite sure how this key issue should be outworked practically.

What follows is my understanding of this oft-neglected area of church life and some thoughts of how it could be more coherently practiced in the Christian communities of which we are a part.

A couple of years ago, I was speaking at a conference in an Asian nation. One morning as I walked towards the conference centre I saw a man ploughing a paddy field, getting it ready for planting rice. Two oxen were pulling the plough and it was obvious that one of them was bigger, stronger and more experienced than the other. The younger animal was yoked together with the 'big guy' and was being trained and equipped for the job. It occurred to me that if I came back there in several years' time, the apprentice would be the one helping another younger ox, one perhaps yet to be born...

Do you remember these words from the Lord?

> *"Take my yoke upon you and learn from me…"*
> *(Matthew 11:29)*

Every believer is first and foremost a follower, an apprentice of Jesus, his disciple. But as we shall see our faith requires not only a primary relationship with him, it also means we live in loving, caring, accountable, shaping friendships with other believers.

Two critical questions for each one of us to answer are:

"Have I been/am I being discipled?"
and "Who am I discipling?"

We are going to explore what this looks like biblically and also how we might work it out practically in our lives.

Given that we have been commissioned by the Lord Jesus Christ to be a disciple and to make disciples, this cannot be seen as optional extras only for the keen Christians.

The Back Story

In the cause of full disclosure, let me explain a little of my own spiritual journey and how it links with the subject of this book. Back in the 1970s, the Charismatic Movement was in full swing across the historic denominations. Just over a decade before I came to faith, God's Spirit had begun to sweep through the Body of Christ in a fresh way. For many believers, the Spirit was blowing away some of the dry orthodoxy of previous times. New worship songs were being written, miracles were being recorded, believers from across the Christian Church would gather for celebration services which went beyond the one hour limit! Charismatic believers were happy and they were clappy!

Five months after having encountered Jesus as my King and Rescuer, I read a book called *Nine O'Clock in the Morning*[1]. It was the true story of an Episcopalian minister and his wife who experienced the baptism in the Holy Spirit. One evening, shortly after reading this, I knelt down in the middle of a football pitch and asked Jesus to fill me up with his presence and his power. And he did. My experience that night empowered me to be able to share my faith boldly and effectively with those I knew or met. The Holy Spirit is the Spirit of mission (Acts 1:8).

---

[1] D.J. Bennett, *Nine O'Clock in the Morning* (Kingsway, 1974).

There is no doubt that what happened through the Charismatic Renewal was generally a wonderful thing. But as with any new move of God there can be aberrations and even abuses which come through flawed, broken and sometimes downright evil human beings. One of the clear downsides at the time was when believers relied too much on their feelings to guide them rather than what God had already made clear in the Bible. Certainly there was a fresh emotional freedom in many churches, but when subjectivism became the guide for morality and how we should live rather than the Word of God, all kinds of spiritual anarchy began to break out.

When it came to the business of guidance and direction, it seemed at the time as if the only thing that counted was an inward sense that "...God has told me..." No checks or balances. No submission to Scripture. And no accountability to pastoral oversight. Many Spirit-filled Christians believed they simply had a hotline to God and this was all that counted. The end result in some places was that "...every man did what was right in his own eyes..." (Judges 17:6). At its worst there were extra-marital affairs, people cheating on their tax forms, massive debt issues, sexual immorality, etc. In the local church there might be a whole bunch of individuals pursuing a personal 'vision' which they strongly believed was from God but which meant it was impossible to hold a cohesive, corporate approach across a congregation.

At this time, what became known as 'the Discipleship Movement' emerged. Networks of churches which today are part of the furniture of the Body of Christ in the UK were viewed at the time as very controversial (e.g. New Frontiers, Pioneer, Salt & Light). Words such as 'accountability', 'submission' and even 'obedience' began to be used. There were accusations of 'heavy shepherding' where church members even had to get permission about what colour to paint their front room, or who to marry. No doubt there was some of this complete excess, although it was difficult to track it down in practice. It does seem however that whenever something is restored by God, the pendulum can be swung too far in the other direction before the happy medium is discovered.

Sally and I were part of this movement for nearly a quarter of a century and experienced very little misuse or abuse. I think a lot of the stories which were reported across the wider Church were a result of Chinese whispers or conspiracy theories! What we were grateful for was a culture of committed relationships in the family of God where generally servant leaders wanted to help you to become all that God intended through encouragement and training. I'm thankful as well that I was confronted from time to time when I needed it and invited to pursue change!

I have a hunch that one of the reasons why we have struggled to fully define discipleship in recent decades and then to work out what it looks like in practice is because of the reaction against what happened through the latter part of the twentieth century with the Discipleship Movement. I also believe that much of what happened then was fine in terms of its orthodoxy; the challenge was more to do with the orthopraxy, i.e. how it was done and its intensity or overkill.

What becomes clear from a simple New Testament word search is that discipleship is a major theme. The word 'Christian(s)' is used only 3 times whilst 'Disciple(s)' is mentioned around 290 times, depending on which translation you use. At the start of his public ministry Jesus called disciples and his final word to them was to make disciples.

The idea and practice of discipleship did not originate with the New Testament or the ministry of Jesus. In Jewish culture there were some committed young men who would attach themselves to a rabbi and live in a very strong relationship so that they could both learn the wisdom and knowledge of the teacher, but also become like him in their lifestyle, practices and values. The Hebrew word for a disciple is *talmid.* Similarly in Greek culture there were disciples of the philosophers and from there we get the word *mathétés* used in the New Testament.

It's important to underline at this point that to be a disciple in the ancient world meant far more than simply being a pupil or student. There is a sense of being relationally connected to the one who is training you and to be 100% committed to the process of whole life learning. The learning is concurrently seen as intellectual, moral, spiritual, imitational and transformational. In the Jewish Mishnah there is a phrase which speaks of being '...covered in the dust of your rabbi', the idea being that, as a disciple, you would follow him so closely that the dust he kicked up as he walked would stick to you. It is no accident therefore that when Jesus called the twelve it was to be "...with him" (Mark 3:14). Gunter Krallman in his book *Mentoring for Mission*[2] calls this 'consociation' and comments:

> *"Jesus viewed discipling as life-transference through the channel of relationships, and not as merely intellectual absorption of certain theoretical precepts."*

We will look at the discipleship style of Jesus later in more detail. For now, it's worth noting that discipleship carries with it the idea of being a loyal apprentice to the one from whom you are learning about the whole of life.

[2] G. Krallman, *Mentoring for Mission* (Authentic Media, 2003).

For Reflection/Discussion

1. Has anyone discipled you? Are you being discipled at present?

2. How did it go, or how is it going? Good, bad and indifferent?

3. What lessons have you learned which you would you put into place if you were shaping someone?

4. As a disciple of Jesus, name one of his teachings which you would like to put into practice more thoroughly.

DISCIPLESHIP AND THE BIBLE
Finding it in the Book

If we take a scan through the whole Bible it's possible to see a number of examples or allusions to discipleship which may help shed light on what's involved.

OLD TESTAMENT

A case could be made for a discipling relationship to have existed between characters such as Abraham and Isaac or David and Solomon. For sure, as we shall see, there is something about a parent/child relationship which inevitably leads to an impartation for good or not-so-good!

There are two particular Old Testament relationships which give some interesting insight into the process.

Moses and Joshua

Joshua is shown to be Moses's assistant or aide and reading between the lines, it's pretty obvious that there was a deep loyalty from Joshua which results in a strong apprenticing from Moses in order to prepare him as the successor in leading God's people. You can see this in various parts of the story.

What discipleship principles can we learn?

- Moses prays hard for Joshua as he battles the Amalekites. It's Moses's prayer along with Joshua's sword which brings victory (Exodus 17).

  The principle of praying for those you are influencing. Discipleship is not simply a human activity but spiritual in nature. If those we train are to succeed in life and service it will not be first and foremost because we have taught them some skills or doctrines: it will be because God has answered our prayers for them!

- Moses takes Joshua up the mountain for a prolonged time in the presence of God (Exodus 24).

  The principle of teaching someone to practice being with God. Jesus has promised to always be with us otherwise we cannot fulfil the Great Commission (Matthew 28:18-20). Our challenge is to remain with him.

- Joshua stays in the tent of meeting even after Moses leaves (Exodus 33).

  The principle of learning intimacy with the Lord. The more we get to know the Lord, the more we will be able to trust him and live by faith. In this instance, the disciple went further than the discipler: not only is this great, it should be the goal!

- Moses encourages and strengthens Joshua to take on the leadership and bring Israel into the Promised Land (Deuteronomy 3:28).

  The principle of calling someone up higher and further than they think they can go. One of the most powerful things you can say to someone in training is 'I believe in you!'

- Moses lays hands on Joshua and commissions him to be his successor (Numbers 27:19, Deuteronomy 34:9).

  The principle of desiring those you train to outdo you in success and fruitfulness.

  Overall, it seems that Moses was involved in calling out of Joshua what was latently in him; wisdom, leadership, wholeheartedness, strength and courage. This is often the role of a discipler.

Elijah and Elisha

There are some keys lessons in this story:

- Elijah invites Elisha to follow him, but makes it relatively easy for him to refuse (1 Kings 19:19-21). The disciple has to make a non-coercive decision to be equipped and trained. If this is not the case, we are in danger of entering into an abusive, controlling relationship

- Elisha was willing to give up his job to follow the prophet (1 Kings 19:21). The disciple needs to count the cost (more on this later).

- Elisha's role was to be Elijah's 'attendant' (1 Kings 19:21). Servanthood is the hallmark of a true disciple. But it is also the hallmark of a true leader (John 13:12-17).

- Elisha stuck by Elijah even when it was emotionally a difficult period for both of them (2 Kings 2:1-12). Stickability and resilience are keys to growth. Disposable relationships are anathema to followers of Jesus.

- When Elijah is taken up, it is instructive to read what Elisha cries out "My father! My father!" (2 Kings 2:12). As we shall see in the New Testament, the purest form of discipleship is parent/child.

- Elisha inherits a double portion of Elijah's spirit (2 Kings 2:9,10). At its best, discipleship results in increase in the life and ministry of the follower.

NEW TESTAMENT

The idea and practice of discipleship was not rare in New Testament times. John the Baptist had disciples (Matthew 11:2, 3). In Acts 5, Gamaliel mentions Theudas and Judas the Galilean both of whom had considerable numbers of followers (disciples?). The Pharisees also had disciples (Mark 2:18).

For the purposes of this chapter I want to point to three models of discipling relationship:

1. JESUS AND THE TWELVE

One of the first things we learn from Jesus is that the taking on of the disciples came about after prolonged prayer. In this case, it was the Lord who had been praying and then he did the choosing. In my view, prayer is an indispensable pre-requisite before a discipling relationship is started, but the choosing, or rather the request/invitation can come from either end!

It might be that during a time of devotions, God speaks to someone about taking on a less mature believer and assisting them in their growth. Even then, wisdom and common sense suggests that this should be checked through with local church leaders before offering the opportunity. Conversely. It may be that a younger believer sees something in a more experienced individual which they aspire to and the approach comes from them. Still, there is some checking out to be done!

A number of people have made the point that when Jesus called the first disciples it consisted of both an invitation and a challenge:

> *"As Jesus walked beside the Sea of Galilee, he saw Simon and his brother Andrew casting a net into the lake, for they were fishermen. [17] 'Come, follow me,' Jesus said, 'and I will send you out to fish for people.' At once they left their nets and followed him." (Mark 1:17,18).*

It's important to be clear at the beginning: what is being offered and what will be expected? Many training relationships have failed on the basis of a lack of clear definition in the first place. Later we will explore how this can be achieved so that misunderstandings are minimized.

As we read through the Gospel accounts, I would suggest we see four approaches to the Jesus style of discipleship:

• "I do it, you watch" = OBSERVATION (Mark 1 – 5)

In Mark's Gospel, after Jesus calls his disciples, they only get to do one thing in the first five chapters and that is simply to get hold of a small boat (3:9); not too difficult a job considering some of them had been fishermen! What we see is the disciples learning from Jesus about healing and deliverance (1:29-34, 40-42, 2:3-12, 3:10-12, 5:1-43), prayer (1:35), legalism (2:18-28, 3:1-6), Kingdom teaching (4:1-34).

• "You do it and report back." = DELEGATION (Luke 9: 1-10)

It's important to notice that when Jesus sends out the twelve on a 'dress rehearsal' of what will happen for the rest of their lives, he gives them very specific instructions. He knows them well and has imparted to them what they will need for the task. It's a narrowly defined activity with a start and finish to it. They would be stretched, but not to breaking point! The disciples no doubt were a little nervous, however they knew that their discipler had given them what they needed to accomplish this activity.

Afterwards there was an opportunity for evaluation and reflection although as we shall see, it was cut short!

• "We do it together." = COLLABORATION (Luke 9: 10-17)

Even at this time of interruption by the crowds, the disciples would have learned something about the approach to ministry. Jesus showed them how important people are. I'm struck by the fact that Jesus did the speaking and the healing until 'late in the afternoon': this would have given the disciples a chance to rest as well.

Then it was time for the next learning module. The feeding of the five thousand men (and who knows how many women and children) showed the disciples that Christ-like care is for the whole person, including the stomach! This miracle is of a different order to healing the sick or casting out demons; it's another step on their journey of growth. Notice the incremental way in which Jesus nurtures their ability to speak words, do works and demonstrate wonders.

• "You do it. I'm going,,," = COMMISSION

The discipleship process would last for around three years before Jesus death, resurrection and ascension to the Father.

There are three key incidents after Jesus was raised from death which shed light on what these followers would end up doing for the rest of their earthly lives:

Firstly, The Great Commission (Matthew 28:18-20)

> *Then Jesus came to them and said, 'All authority in heaven and on earth has been given to me. Therefore go and make disciples of all nations, baptising them in the name of the Father and of the Son and of the Holy Spirit, and teaching them to obey everything I have commanded you. And surely I am with you always, to the very end of the age.'*

The emphasis in Christ's words is on making disciples as we go to all people groups on the planet. Baptism is an essential part of the process as is teaching the new followers the words and ways of Jesus and how to walk as he did in their own context. There will be a lot more to explore about this, but it's worth making the point here that the Commission is not to make converts but rather disciples. I still meet people who think that because they repeated a formula of words some time ago (commonly known as 'the sinner's prayer') they are now safe for eternity even if they choose to live a profligate life.

Second, The 'Greatest Commission' (John 20:21,22)

> *Again Jesus said, 'Peace be with you! As the Father has sent me, I am sending you.' And with that he breathed on them and said, 'Receive the Holy Spirit.'*

In his book *Missional God: Missional Church*[3], Ross Hastings suggests that these words could be termed 'The Greatest Commission' since it hints strongly at the essential nature of the Trinity as a Community of sending love. The biblical idea is that the Church's mandate to make disciples flows directly from the heart of a God who loves people. He therefore was not willing to stop short of visiting this world in the person of Jesus of Nazareth and ultimately sacrificing himself so that the missional Spirit of God could join with Father and Son in sending the Church to facilitate others coming into relationship with their Creator. Wow. Just, wow!

---

[3] R. Hastings, *Missional God: Missional Church* (IVP, 2012).

Thirdly, The Kingdom Seminar (Acts 1:3)

> *"After his suffering, he presented himself to them*
> *and gave many convincing proofs that he was alive.*
> *He appeared to them over a period of forty days*
> *and spoke about the kingdom of God."*

Can you imagine it? A six week seminar from the risen Lord focused on one subject; the main subject of his teaching during his earthly ministry! Wouldn't you have liked to have been there?

The frustrating thing is that Luke doesn't tell us what he said; we are left hanging. But here is a thought...if you had been there and had taken on board what he said, and then you had watched him ascend back to heaven, and you had later received the promised Holy Spirit on the Day of Pentecost, what would you have spent the rest of your life doing?

My suggestion is that those first disciples would have put into practice what they had been taught, not just in the previous three years, but particularly what they had learnt from the glorified, risen Lord over those forty days. Why would they do anything else, particularly now they had been empowered to do it? Perhaps then we can do some detective work by extrapolating backwards from the twenty seven chapters which follow in the Book of Acts and imagining what Jesus taught his followers based on what they actually did.

What is easily discoverable is that they (eventually) took the Gospel out to all parts of the then-known world. Wherever the apostles went they preached about Jesus, God usually confirming their words with signs, wonders and miracles. As people turned to Christ they were formed together as new communities of Jesus followers and churches were formed made up of disciples.

Essentially, the Kingdom of God is manifested as more and more people surrender to the kingly rule of Jesus and the signs of how things will be when Christ finally returns are seen right here, right now through healings, deliverance from powers of darkness and lives transformed to become more like Jesus. Wonderful! In essence, that's the story of Acts!

2. PAUL AND TIMOTHY

The closest form of discipleship which can be imagined is a parent-child relationship. When Paul first met Timothy in Lystra in Acts 16, it's clear that his mother was a believer but his dad wasn't. We have no clear idea what kind of relationship Timothy had with his father, but he is never mentioned by name and Paul writes about the faith of both his mom and his grandmother which is now resident in the son/grandson (2 Tim 1:5). You don't have to read too much between the lines to realise that in a spiritual and emotional way, Paul undertook this paternal role. There are a number of occasions in Paul's letters where he refers to Timothy as his son (1 Tim 1:2, 1:18. 2 Tim 1:2, 2:1. Phil 2:22).

As a good father, Paul was concerned to be an example to his son when it came to Christian living and to discharging ministry. So he writes:

> *"You, however, know all about my teaching, my way of life, my purpose, faith, patience, love, endurance…"*
> *(2 Tim 3:10)*

Added to this, because there was an integration between who Paul was and how he lived, and because of the close relationship they seemed to have, Paul is quite directive in his letters concerning how Timothy should conduct himself, telling him, for example, to

> *"…watch your life and doctrine closely…" (1 Tim 4:16).*

Like any good father, Paul does not want to 'mollycoddle' his son. There is no sense of wrapping him up in cotton wool. In fact one of the first tasks Timothy gets is to go to Ephesus and sort out some of the aberrant teachers there – no easy job! (1 Tim 1:3-7).

As Paul comes towards the end of his life, he refers to Timothy as his 'fellow worker' (Romans 16:21). Again, fathers are thrilled if or when their children do even better than they have done: there is no sense of this being a competition.

I remember very few of the sermons I've heard through the years, although I'm sure they have done me good: I have a similar issue with the meals I've eaten! One message I do remember was back in the very early 1980s from a pastor named Charles Simpson from Mobile, Alabama. His title was 'success and succession'. What I remember was his thesis; that the mark of our success is how many fruitful people we leave behind. I guess that is the mark of a healthy family!

We are living at a time when there are so many parentless, dare I say (given that in broken marriages, most kids stay mainly with mum), fatherless people in our world. In another context, Paul wrote:

> *"Even if you had ten thousand guardians in Christ, you do not have many fathers, for in Christ Jesus I became your father through the gospel."(1Cor 4:15)*

We face similar challenges in the 21st Century. May we be able to find spiritual parents and become spiritual parents to so many who have been spiritually orphaned.

3. JESUS AND THE FATHER

In finishing off this chapter, I wanted to point out that Jesus of Nazareth was a disciple!

I like the story in Luke 2 when his human parents lost him for three whole days. Understandably, his mum was flustered when they retrieved him. It's worth noting what happened over the next several years:

> *"Then he went down to Nazareth with them and was obedient to them...And Jesus grew in wisdom and stature, and in favour with God and man.*
> *(Luke 2:51, 52)*

There's no suggestion of him being rebellious or 'adolescent', the opposite in fact. But even in his sinless humanity, there was growth that took place as he submitted both to his human parents and to his Heavenly Father.

Later on in his adult life, Jesus would clarify that the things he did and the words he spoke were both from his Father (John 5:19, 8:38, 12:50). Not that he was an automaton or robot. Jesus could have chosen his own will against the Father's will but perfectly chose not to do so (Luke 22:42).

As in all things, Jesus is the ultimate example: a human being who voluntarily chose to place himself under the tutelage of his Heavenly Father so that his life freely offered up would produce something extremely wonderful, namely the salvation of the world. This obedient disciple undid all that was lost through Adam's rebellious action so that we could once again know the experience of friendship with God. Iranaeus of Lyon, one of the early church fathers called this 'recapitulation', the righting through Jesus's obedience of all that was made wrong through Adam's sin.

As I write these words I am filled with overwhelming gratitude to the one who was obedient even to the point of death on the cross (Philippians 2:8). Thank you, Jesus!

For Reflection/Discussion

1. Which principle strikes you most forcibly from the relationship between Moses and Joshua?

2. What particular lesson stands out to you from the story of Elijah and Elisha?

3. In reading about how Jesus trained the disciples, what was highlighted for you?

4. To what degree do you have a sense of being 'sent' by God into your workplace or your main sphere of activity? How does this show itself?

21ST CENTURY DISCIPLESHIP
The Challenge of Contemporary Culture

I was only nine months old when Harold MacMillan, the Prime Minister of the United Kingdom at the time, famously observed:

> *"...most of our people have never had it so good..."*
> *(July 1957)*

The post-war economic boom meant that rationing was a thing of the past, there was plenty of food in the shops including bananas and oranges! An increasing number of families could afford to buy a car - as long as it was black or white. You could even get a television – as long as it was black and white!

The demise of Christendom (culture shaped by Christian morality and values) had already begun, even though it was slow at first. The rise of Materialism (culture shaped by what I have and what I own) was becoming more and more evident.

In the six decades or more since, there have been massive moves in Western culture. Christendom has almost entirely collapsed and Materialism has given birth to a child; Consumerism.

The Consumer mind set of the twenty first century person affects our whole worldview. Someone has commented that the new religion is shopping – *"Tesco ergo sum* – I shop therefore I am". It has become the cultural water in which we swim. We don't know any other way of being or acting. In our Consumerist World we are offered not only 'stuff' but a massive range of 'stuff'. No longer does it have to be either black or white; you can have any colour, any flavour, any shape, any size...the consumer is king.

The effect on discipleship has been the rise of the 'Consumer Christian'. It would not be an overstatement to suggest that all believers are affected by this to a greater or lesser degree.

Think about it...on what basis have you decided to belong to your local church? For the majority of us it's to do with the style of worship, the preaching/teaching ability of the pastor, the comfort of the seats, the quality of the after-service coffee, the pastoral support offered, the 'feel good' factor.

Which Bible do you use? King James or the Passion? Or any one of the many other versions which are now available? Do you prefer Bethel worship or Hillsong? Or are you 'old school' and still partial to Graham Kendrick? Do you watch God TV or TBN UK? Songs of Praise? None of the above? You see, we are saturated by choice.

One more thing. I once heard an American minister, Dennis Peacocke describe what he termed 'the Pulpit Conspiracy'. He outlined the kind of transaction which takes place in a subliminal fashion between a preacher and the congregation. His point was that the people will sit and listen to the sermon, smile, nod, even let out an occasional 'Yes!' or 'Hallelujah!' But often they have no intention of doing anything with what they have heard. Now this is an exaggeration of the truth, but in my experience there is something in it.

Jesus told the story of the wise and foolish builders who built on different foundations. The reason that the foolish man didn't stand the time of testing was not because he hadn't heard the word of the Lord; it was because, unlike the wise man, he hadn't put it into practice (Matthew 7:24-27).

We are spiritual consumers who, without realising it, have postured ourselves as paying for goods and services. If we don't like what we are being offered or we are encouraged to move out of our comfort zone, we may well take our business elsewhere or cease our involvement altogether. There are great swathes of believers who have become what would be described technically as 'de-churched'. Now, how on earth do you encourage someone to follow a discipleship pathway if the only time spiritual interaction occurs is when the person sits in front of a preacher on an occasional Sunday, or if he/she is disconnected from the people of God?

So Consumerism mitigates against true biblical discipleship. But there are a few other 21st Century cultural markers which also act as brakes:

• When rights trump responsibilities

At their best, human rights flow out from a Creator who, in the words of the USA Constitution bestowed certain rights on every human being. In the 1940s, The Universal Declaration of Human Rights massively expanded on this and most fair minded human beings would agree with most, if not all of it. The problem arises when as an individual I perceive 'rights' as the freedom to do what I want rather than what I ought to do. Discipleship presupposes that I will from time to time surrender up my personal rights and act in such a way that someone else receives benefit at my expense. In biblical terms, I choose to be my brother's keeper (Genesis 4:9).

• When personal autonomy trumps Truth

Where do we find our authority for the way we live our lives and what we believe? More than ever, we look inside ourselves to find 'our truth' rather than any external plumbline. 'What I think' becomes more relevant and powerful than anything proposed by an institution or 'the experts'. This has a detrimental effect on any discipling matrix if we believe that no one can tell me what to do. It is the case, of course, that any moral/spiritual journey which is imposed or forced on another cannot be the way of Jesus. Nevertheless, the need for humble submission to unchanging biblical ways and disciplines is foundational for someone to experience Christian growth.

• When instant trumps investment

We are living in a debt-ridden society. Our culture fights against the idea of there being any delay between wanting something (or someone?) and actually having it. We 'stick it on the credit card' in order to gain immediate gratification. So many items can be had at the press of a button or the presentation of a piece of plastic.

If you, like me, are keen on sport, you will know that when you watch a top athlete perform there is a long backstory. They may have a natural ability but to do what they do presupposes that they have spent many days, weeks, months training to reach the level they are now at. In a similar way, there is no such thing as instant maturity; in fact that is an oxymoron! If we want to maximise our lives as followers of Jesus it's imperative that we invest now with the future in mind. We are saved by grace, which is the wonderful truth of the Gospel (Ephesians 2:8, 9), But faith without works is dead (James 2:14-26).

• When feelings trump the will

As far back as the early 1970s, Della Reese released the Northern Soul single *'If it feels good, do it'* which became a smash hit. She was expressing what had become the prevailing approach to life, freedom to do whatever your emotions tell you (within certain legally controlled limits, usually).

One of the areas which the twelve who followed Jesus had to learn to master was exactly this. Remember John and James were nicknamed 'Sons of thunder' because they had some temper issues (Mark 3:17). This becomes evident when they wanted to call down fire to destroy a community which barred the way to Jesus (Luke 9:54). Even after three years with the Lord, Peter showed how weak-willed he became when he was emotionally exhausted (Luke 22:45); he ended up denying that he even knew Christ (Luke 22:56-62).

Contrast the disciples with Jesus in Gethsemane. On an emotional level, the last thing he wanted was to go through the agony of crucifixion and yet he chose the Father's will (Luke 22:42). One of the marks of moving towards spiritual maturity will be the ability to say 'no' to those things we need to say 'no' to and the ability to say 'yes' to the will of God, even when it feels difficult.

Two key scriptures speak loudly into these 21st century challenges. First of all, Jesus said:

> *"No one can serve two masters. Either you will hate*
> *the one and love the other, or you will be devoted*
> *to the one and despise the other. You cannot serve both*
> *God and money."(Luke 16:13)*

It's almost as if the Lord is saying that in the same way that God has a life and a power of His own, distinct from anything else, so it can be with money and therefore also, 'stuff'. In this sense, money and what it has the potential to provide is not a neutral medium, but more a god, certainly if we end up serving it rather than our Creator.

Secondly, the apostle Paul writes:

> *"Therefore, I urge you, brothers and sisters, in view of God's mercy, to offer your bodies as a living sacrifice, holy and pleasing to God – this is your true and proper worship. Do not conform to the pattern of this world, but be transformed by the renewing of your mind. Then you will be able to test and approve what God's will is – his good, pleasing and perfect will."(Romans 12:1, 2).*

Wow! There is so much here, but for the sake of the focus in this chapter, let me offer this...

We choose sacrifice on the basis of 'God's mercy'. Up until this point in his letter, Paul has mainly been explaining why Jesus died and the benefits which are given to us because of the cross. So, Jesus freely gave himself up for us; what should be our response?

Then Paul gives us a massive clue about how we can live our lives in a counter-cultural way, by our thinking being changed. The word translated 'repentance' in the New Testament means to change your mind. The idea here is that if we change our thinking, our worldview, we will end up moving in a different direction in our lives. It's worth mentioning that Paul has already counselled the Romans to give their bodies to God so that there would not be a contradiction between what they believed in their minds and what they did with their flesh!

The call to discipleship is radical. It requires that whenever the culture around us conflicts with following Jesus, we choose Jesus. It means that we have to be more 'savvy' about the world we live in and, where necessary we will need to swim against the prevailing currents and actually invite others to do so as well. The end result of doing so will mean a great personal adventure for us and as more and more disciples choose Christ over culture, the course of the whole Universe can be changed. Which takes us onto the next chapter...

For Reflection/Discussion

Review this chapter and as you do so write down your thoughts under these three headings:

1. **Question Mark** – is there anything I have read which I don't fully understand or that leaves me questioning some aspect of my life?

2. **Candle** – What has been illuminated to me as I have read this? What am I now seeing more clearly? Were there any moments when I 'saw' something for the first time or when I was reminded of something I'd forgotten?

3. **Exclamation Mark!** – At what points did I feel challenged about how I am approaching life as a Jesus follower? What will I do about these things?

THE DISCIPLESHIP JOURNEY-
WHERE ARE WE GOING?

Personal and Universal Transformation

I think it was on a TV travel programme that I first heard someone make the point that the important thing about travel is not the destination, it's all about the journey. Now what is the point of being on a road to Nowhere? Of course there will be experiences to be had and miles to be covered on the journey; but where does it end? Where are we going?

It seems to me that from God's perspective there are two ultimate ends to the discipleship journey, if it is possible to have two ultimates!

The first is **the personal destination** which God has for each one of us.

I don't know if you have a 'life verse' meaning a particular part of the Bible which is really significant for you and has become the 'go to' passage or verse which guides or encourages you in a positive way. Many people received such a scripture when they were baptised or when they became an official member of a church, and that's great. For me, I think the whole Bible is pretty good! But if you push me for one place to turn it would be Romans 8:29:

> *"For those God foreknew he also predestined to be conformed to the image of his Son, that he might be the firstborn among many brothers and sisters."*

I'm reminded that not only has God saved me from some terrible things but he has also saved me for a purpose which is to transform me more and more into the likeness of Jesus of Nazareth.

John Mark Comer has helpfully suggested that a disciple will be someone who increasingly will:

- Be with Jesus

- Become like Jesus

- Do what Jesus did[4]

Dallas Willard describes it as

"...how Jesus would live my life if he were me."[5]

These two descriptions are very helpful in setting out the direction of the journey we need to head out on, and what a personal adventure it is! It will be evidenced in the development of our values, attitudes, habits and all-round moral character.

In terms of our personalities, well, we are all different; part of God's great kaleidoscope of humanity. There are occasions when someone who has been an introvert becomes far more outgoing when they meet Jesus and vice versa, but this is very much the exception rather than the rule and there is no sense in which one personality type is better than another!

We are called to be holy women and men (1 Peter 1:16, 2:9). Sometimes we misunderstand what it means to be holy, supposing that we are meant to be killjoys who look like we are perpetually sucking on lemons. But Jesus was full of 'the oil of joy' (Hebrews 1:9)! He told the best stories, enjoyed eating and drinking and the fact that little children wanted to hang out with him tells you that he was a fun guy. And he was the purest human being ever to walk on the planet.

Added to our moral character and integrity, we will be disciples who develop the gifts that God has given us so that we can fulfil our unique purpose in this life. There are natural abilities as well as spiritual gifts to develop and I would suggest that Jesus had both sorts. It is the case that we don't read much about his natural

---

[4] https://johnmarkcomer.com/#about

[5] D. Willard, *The Divine Conspiracy* (Fount, 1998) p68

talents in the New Testament, but don't forget he was a carpenter for the majority of his life and, I am confident, he was excellent at dovetail joints!

Spiritual gifts come to us from the Giver once we are connected to Him, the Holy Spirit. In fact, have you ever noticed that Jesus is not recorded as doing even one miraculous or supernatural act until he was filled with the Holy Spirit? (Luke 4). Now, if that was the case for the Son of God, if even he needed to be 'filled in order to function', how much more will that be true for us? In later chapters we will look at the receiving and development of spiritual gifts in our lives.

Essentially then, I propose that if we are growing in Christlikeness, we need to recognise the need for three increasingly evident hallmarks. The first would be to do with our **moral purity**. Sometimes I think Christians believe they have to lock themselves away from those who don't follow Jesus if they are to remain clean. Well, Jesus hung out with tax gatherers, publicans and prostitutes. And he never sinned.

Two things are worth remembering here: God has given us all that we need for life and godliness (2 Peter 1:3) but He doesn't want us to be stupid. What I mean is that we are all 'works in progress', and some contexts might be overwhelmingly difficult for one believer to remain loyal to Jesus whereas another Christian could handle it well. For example, I would not recommend a brand new Jesus follower who has just exited drug addiction to go alone back to a crack house where a lot of his previous buddies are still using. Discipleship is a process. These days there are places I can go and people I can be with and even though they may be involved in unwholesome things, it doesn't cross my mind to join in. It would have been far more difficult when I was a baby believer! I think you get the point. God will not allow you to be tempted beyond what you are able to bear (1 Corinthians 10:13), so don't allow yourself to be either.

The second hallmark will be evidenced by the manifestation of **spiritual power.** I can still remember the Sunday evening service which I was taking in a quite formal church where the preacher led everything and did everything. I was going to preach on Jesus being the Way, the Truth and the Life, so in the middle of the service I turned to John 14 and began to read out the passage. As I flicked over the page to continue I read these words:

> *"Very truly I tell you, whoever believes in me will do the works I have been doing, and they will do even greater things than these, because I am going to the Father."*
> *(John 14:12)*

Now I had read those words of Jesus before, many times, but at that moment it suddenly hit me that as well as speaking words from God, I was also supposed to do His works, in this context meaning healings and miracles. This became the start of a fresh journey with the Lord which still continues of course. I'm challenged by the fact that if I am supposed to emulate Jesus then I will want to experience his power released in and through me in the form of signs and wonders.

Thirdly I recognise in Christ a person of **emotional stability**. Jesus wasn't afraid to show his emotions but he wasn't controlled by them. This is clear when you read about his righteous indignation when he threw the money changers out of the temple. Mark tells us that he had seen what was happening the previous day and had 'slept on it' before coming back and, without losing his temper, inviting them to leave! (Mark 11:11, 15-17). He didn't mind having a laugh; he told some really funny stories about camels and shepherds. And he wasn't afraid to cry, weeping at the tomb of his friend Lazarus (John 11:35).

So these three Christ-like qualities have been about our **personal** journey towards being more and more like the Lord.

The second ultimate journey's end is **cosmic**! Or even **eschatological**! Now this is a tad deep, so hold on...

God created humans and made them in his image. To begin with, the Lord could see himself perfectly reflected in Adam and Eve. Then came their rebellion recorded in Genesis 3. Now when God looked at humanity, it was a distorted image which was reflected back to Him.

Throughout the Old Testament, God chooses a people in which his image could be restored, the nation of Israel, but they constantly rebel. Even the best of them, King David, a man after God's own heart (Acts 13:22) messes up morally and militarily.

It's not until we get to the New Testament that there is a human being who is 'the image of the invisible God' (Colossians 1:15); someone who could honestly declare that to see him is to see God perfectly reflected (John 14:9). Jesus, writes Paul, is the second Adam who puts right all that was made wrong through the first Adam's sin and rebellion – read Romans 5!

Now, back to Romans 8:29. Jesus is, in Hebrew culture, the privileged first born, but notice that there are going to be many siblings – you, me and all the other believers! Each one of us will be reflections of our Heavenly Father.

There will come a time when the full number of disciples have come to God from every people group on Earth, and then 'the end' will come (Matthew 24:14). What will 'the end' look like? In short, God, in Jesus, has begun a New Creation to replace the old one which has been subject to decay, disease, death and frustration (Romans 8:18-22). The big difference is that God is recreating everything in reverse order! The original creation began with the heavens and the earth and finished on day six with the making of humans. In this New Creation, God has begun with humans (2 Corinthians 5:17) and it will end with a new heavens and a new earth (Revelation 21:1). Wow!

As I'm sure you have worked out, this overview shows the critical importance of disciple making. We need to reach those who are far from God and enable them to become fully devoted followers of Jesus. The final result of this will be God's Kingdom coming on earth as well as in Heaven; a kingdom of righteousness, peace and joy in the Holy Spirit (Romans 14:17).

So the journey is exciting, but the destination is cosmic!

For Reflection/Discussion

1. Do you have a 'life verse'? Or a particular piece of the Bible which means a lot to you? If so, what is it and why does it mean so much?

2. Given the three qualities of Jesus's person, how would you say you measure up on a scale of 1 – 10? (Don't feel condemned! This is simply a way of calling each one of us up higher and to go further.)

   • Moral purity

   • Spiritual power

   • Emotional stability

   What would need to happen for you to grow in these areas?

3. In light of God's eternal purposes for the Universe, explain why our individual growth is so important.

THE COST OF DISCIPLESHIP

Do You Really Want To Do This?

There is often a caricature of the basis by which someone becomes a Jesus follower. It was well summed up in the words of a little ditty we used to sing when I was in a church youth group back in the Jurassic age...

> *"If you want joy, real joy, wonderful joy,*
> *Let Jesus come into your heart.*
> *If you want joy, real joy, wonderful joy,*
> *Let Jesus come into your heart.*
> *Your sins He'll take away,*
> *Your night He'll turn to day.*
> *Your heart He'll make over anew*
> *And then come in to stay.*
> *If you want joy, real joy, wonderful joy,*
> *Let Jesus come into your heart."*

Now, you may be wondering "what is the problem?" The answer is that these words are close enough to the truth to be dangerous!

It is the case that there are experiences of deep joy, awesome peace and wonderful love in following the Lord. There are also seasons of trial, difficulty and hardship. Added to this, there is very little in the New Testament about 'inviting Jesus into your heart' even though I'm reasonably OK with the word picture being offered.

Perhaps a change of lyrics?

> *"If you want scars, real scars, alongside the joy,*
> *Surrender your life to King Jesus.*
> *If you want challenge, tough challenge, together with peace,*
> *Choose submission to Christ the King"*

Same tune, but more accurate to the reality of authentic Christian living!

There came a time in Jesus's ministry when he was attracting shedloads of followers. Maybe they had been attracted by the way he spoke and the stories he told. No doubt the miracles and healings were a crowd puller. Jesus was becoming a Superstar! Astonishingly, it was at this point that he turned to the large gathering and told them:

> *"If anyone comes to me and does not hate father and mother, wife and children, brothers and sisters—yes, even their own life—such a person cannot be my disciple. And whoever does not carry their cross and follow me cannot be my disciple.*
>
> *"Suppose one of you wants to build a tower. Won't you first sit down and estimate the cost to see if you have enough money to complete it? For if you lay the foundation and are not able to finish it, everyone who sees it will ridicule you, saying, 'This person began to build and wasn't able to finish.'*
>
> *"Or suppose a king is about to go to war against another king. Won't he first sit down and consider whether he is able with ten thousand men to oppose the one coming against him with twenty thousand? If he is not able, he will send a delegation while the other is still a long way off and will ask for terms of peace. In the same way, those of you who do not give up everything you have cannot be my disciples." (Luke 14:26-33)*

Jesus was a realist. He knew that many of those who had joined the 'Jesus Bandwagon' would not last the pace or the journey. So he unpacks the cost.

- Where will your loyalty be? Will you choose family over faith? Of course he is using hyperbole here – exaggeration to drive it home. Anyone who has truly embraced the Christian way of life actually discovers that they care more about other people, not less! And we know that the Great Command is to love God and people. It's a question of priority: will those we are closest to become idols? In other words will we treat something good as if it were God?

- Two thousand years ago in the Roman Empire, if you saw someone carrying a cross you knew what the end would be; crucifixion. So the invitation is simple – come and die! Give up your own ambitions and plans for your life; die to them. It's only then that you can pick up the resurrection life which Jesus offers. Someone once said that the best way to live in God's world is God's way, but you do need to give up the old 'me life'.

  It's important to note that earlier on, Jesus has taught about taking up the cross 'daily' (Luke 9:23). In other words, this decision to surrender all to him is not a one-off event but a daily choice. You see, God is really good at doing resurrections, but so are we. You will have noticed I'm sure that when we choose to allow our old self to live once more, it gets messy, dark and dirty. Conversely, dead people don't claim rights for themselves. Dead people don't give in to temptation. When we die to ourselves, then we can truly live a Christ-honouring life.

- Most of us will have had the embarrassing experience of starting something that we couldn't finish. Often nobody else or very few others found out what happened, but what if lots of people knew? What if it was a big project and they laughed out loud at our foolishness or lack of foresight? Jesus is saying 'count the cost!' Don't try Christianity as if it were a hobby which you can simply take or leave as it suits you!

- Lastly, he verbally hits them with potentially the knock-out blow. It's really an underlining of what he's just said: if you are not prepared to give this adventure everything, settle for a peaceful life in contrast to what could have been epic but really difficult.

You may have heard the story about the hen and the pig who were chatting in the farmyard one day and discussing how to solve the problem of world hunger.

Suddenly the hen exclaimed "I know what to do! We'll feed them all on bacon and eggs!" The pig looked really troubled, so the hen asked "What's wrong with you? It's a great plan!"

"Ah," said the pig "It's OK for you. You'll only have to make an offering. For me it will require total commitment..."

If we are going to be in this, we will need to be proverbial pigs, not hens!

All of the above is very sobering and it's totally appropriate to ask "why would I ever choose such a difficult path for my life?" Here's the answer.

Jesus told two very short parables:

> *"The kingdom of heaven is like treasure hidden in a field. When a man found it, he hid it again, and then in his joy went and sold all he had and bought that field."*

> *"Again, the kingdom of heaven is like a merchant looking for fine pearls. When he found one of great value, he went away and sold everything he had and bought it." (Matthew 13:44-46)*

I'm reminded of the day I got married to Sally: Saturday 25th August 1979. The organ began to play and the congregation stood. I looked back down the aisle as this gorgeous young woman advanced towards me, her dad giving me threatening looks (not really!).

On reflection, I was giving up so much on that day; time, space, a certain set of freedoms, my autonomy; even the sole use of the TV remote controls! The truth is that none of that crossed my mind. All I could feel was the joy and delight of being united with Sally. I was making promises to go forward in this exclusive relationship and not turn back. I was delighted to do so and still am.

In a similar way, becoming a fully-fledged disciple of Jesus depends on saying 'no' to some things and approaches to life in order to say 'yes' to him. So it's costly, but look what you get in return: Treasure! An invaluable pearl! The astonishing privilege of being a child of God and a close friendship with the benevolent King of the Universe! From that perspective, it's a bargain.

Jim Elliot was a missionary who set out to reach the Quechua Indians of Ecuador with the Gospel. Very early on he was speared to death on a remote river beach. In the years that followed many of the Quechua became believers. The quote Elliot is most famous for is this:

> *"He is no fool who gives what he cannot keep to gain that which he cannot lose."*[6]

Yes, there is much sacrifice in being a disciple. It takes some living, but I know that I want to have a life of challenge and one which makes a difference rather than to simply freefall through the years and finish either separated from my loving Creator for eternity or making it into eternal life but only just '...as one escaping through the flames...'(1 Corinthians 3:15). Dallas Willard was clearly right when he observed:

> *"...The cost of non-discipleship is greater than the cost of discipleship."*[7]

Who in their right mind wants to inherit eternal life by the skin of their teeth?

Perhaps the following has been implicit in this chapter, so to finish let me spell it out. The cross of Christ was where the ultimate cost was paid. Jesus was crucified so that we could know what it is to be forgiven and reconciled to God, that's totally true. But what else? Paul writes these words:

---

[6] E. Elliot, *The Shadow of the Almighty* (Authentic Classics, 2005).

[7] D. Willard, *The Divine Conspiracy* (Fount, 1998).

> *"...we are convinced that one died for all, and therefore all died. And he died for all, that those who live should no longer live for themselves but for him who died for them and was raised again." (2 Corinthians 5:14, 15).*

The cross stands front and centre in the Christian faith and, when we have an authentic revelation of all that Jesus did for each one of us, then no sacrifice or cost on our part is too great.

The most obvious reading of the two short parables mentioned earlier is that you or I are the person who finds the treasure or the fine pearl. But alternatively, what about if the person searching is actually the Lord? He thought that having found us, we were so very important and valuable to him that he was willing to go and pay with all that he had so that we could become his possession. And that is what he did. In reality, I belong to Jesus. He has bought me with his precious blood, his life. On that basis from my side, 'cost' and 'sacrifice' pretty much lose their meaning.

Thank you Lord Jesus for giving it all up for me. Now, it's my turn...

For Reflection/Discussion

1. We can make idols out of other people or things. What would be the biggest area of temptation for you?

2. What do you find you have to 'crucify' in your life regularly in order to live for Jesus?

3. What are the biggest benefits for you which result from a life more surrendered to the Lord?

DISCIPLESHIP AND THE GOSPEL
If It's Not Missional, It's Not Discipleship

It's the most natural thing in the world to share good news.

I still remember the day my granddaughter was born. I was grabbing a coffee from the drive-thru at a fast food restaurant. As I pulled up at the hole in the wall and wound my window down I began to excitedly tell the server all about the arrival of Sia Rose. In all honesty he didn't seem very interested either in her name or her birth weight or about the cute little cardigan recently knitted for her by her granny. I didn't care: I just kept telling him about our new baby as the queue of cars behind me became more and more irritated.

As I'm sure you know, the word 'Gospel' simply means 'good news'. And we have the very best news for human beings who are far away from God, still lost and actually spiritually dead in their sins (Ephesians 2:1). We have got something to broadcast about how the Creator of all things loved people so much that He wasn't willing to stand on one side and watch us march off like a bunch of lemmings heading for a long drop. He didn't want us to spend eternity separated from his glorious presence. That's why he visited this sin-sick planet in the person of Jesus of Nazareth. Jesus showed us in a human framework what our Creator is really like. He demonstrated his amazing grace to the final degree by sacrificing himself in our place on the cross, taking the blame for our rebellion and wrongdoing. Now, because Jesus died for us, we can experience forgiveness for our past. Because God raised Jesus from the dead, we can know that the power of death has been defeated and we can enjoy the remarkable privilege of friendship with our Creator. If that isn't the most scintillating good news you've ever heard, I don't know what is!

It's a strange thing then that given that this is the best news ever, we tend towards reluctance in sharing it with others.

Mike Pilavachi, the founder and leader of Soul Survivor and all-round good guy tweeted the following:

"The greatest evangelistic tool we have? Disciples.
Men and women who look and sound and smell like Jesus.
Techniques, gimmicks and shows are never going to
do it."

Sometimes I hear a speaker talk about 'missional discipleship'; is there any other kind? To be a disciple presupposes that you are committed to fishing for people. I've also heard it said that we need to leave evangelism to the evangelists since it's their gift. If that were the case, the task of taking the Gospel effectively to every people group on Earth would never be completed. Simple maths tells you that this is the case.

Imagine an incredibly gifted international evangelist recording 100,000 decisions for Christ every week. This would mean that he would see more than five million declarations of faith every year. Now imagine 'Joe Bloggs Christian' who reaches one other person each year and trains the new believer to do the same. At the end of year one, there would be two disciples. At the end of year two there would be four. On this basis, leaving out births and deaths (!!!), the whole world would be disciples of Jesus Christ within thirty three years. The highly successful international evangelist would have seen around two percent of the world population making decisions but with little certainty about whether they have moved along a discipleship pathway.

Now of course there are all sorts of 'Yes, but...' points to be made from this, but it's a challenge even if the maths isn't entirely accurate.

What Stops Us?

After many years of asking Christians what causes them to suffer 'evangelistic inertia', I have come up with these five most common issues:

• Lack of Boldness – Get Confident!

Fear usually causes paralysis or at best, reluctance! When it comes to sharing our faith, we are concerned about being rejected or misunderstood or misrepresented. If we choose to say nothing, there is no fear to overcome! The truth is that the fear is more to do with how we imagine someone might react to us taking an opportunity to share the love of God rather than the reality. Generally the worst that happens is that we are met with a burst of indifference and actually, many people in the right context are interested to know how and why we have 'become religious'.

It's worth saying as well that if a person does react negatively they are not so much rejecting you but rather the worldview which you hold. We need to be a little more thick-skinned!

Now boldness is not the same thing as being obnoxious or rude, but it does require us to step up and step out.

I'm very glad that 365 times in the Bible, God says 'don't be afraid!' It means every day is covered except, of course, February 29th when you can be as fearful and timid as you like...

• Lack of Knowledge – Get Educated!

If I asked you to explain God's Good News message to me in a jargon-free, coherent way and to do it in less than a couple of minutes, could you do that?

What about some of the Big Questions which many perceive as hurdles standing in the way of faith in Christ? Could you give a clear answer to the main objections?

Do you have a decent overview of how Scripture hangs together?

If the answer to any of these questions is 'no' or you are hesitant, there are books to read, courses to take and conversations to have with those who have already trodden these paths.

• Lack of Skills – Get Trained!

Tim Keller, a well-known Christian leader, thinker and evangelist often fields questions from sceptics at the end of a meeting where he has been speaking. I remember listening to him talk about how he learnt to do this; his simple answer was 'by doing it!' He described how he often went back to his accommodation afterwards and reflected on how he might do better next time. You can learn a lot in a classroom about the skills of active listening and reflective questioning, etc., and it's helpful to role play with others. But more is learnt when you put into practice the theory and learn on the job.

One of the great skills of sharing the Gospel is not simply to answer the question but to answer the questioner. This takes a mix of grace alongside the truth! You will have heard that you can win an argument but lose a friend. The soft skills of kindness, empathy and grace are just as important as having all the intellectual answers.

• Lack of Friends – Get Some!

When we begin to seriously pursue faith in Jesus it takes up time, energy and resources. The challenge is how to do this without abandoning our existing friends who are still far from God. It is not unusual a few years after becoming a disciple to realise that you have lost meaningful contact with your previous non-Christian friends. If this happens it becomes very difficult to be involved in fruitful witness.

Almost everyone who comes to know the Lord does so through the agency of someone they already know. It's not very often the case that 'cold' evangelism reaps a sustainable harvest and it's even rarer that someone has a salvation download from Heaven without any human being involved.

• Lack of Care – Get God's Heart!

If we're honest with ourselves and honest with God, sometimes the reason we are not involved in sharing the love of God is simply because we don't care, or at least we don't care enough.

Let's face it; life is busy. We have all got plenty going on and the thought of having to carve out time to hang out with irreligious people who are just not like me or you, can be a step too far. Our emotional bank accounts are already pretty close to being overdrawn and now there's other people who require something from me. No thank you!

What Will Motivate Us?

Through the years there have been two passages in the New Testament which have helped me a lot when I have been feeling non-zealous about reaching out. Here is the first:

> *"When he saw the crowds, he had compassion on them, because they were harassed and helpless, like sheep without a shepherd. Then he said to his disciples, 'The harvest is plentiful but the workers are few. Ask the Lord of the harvest, therefore, to send out workers into his harvest field.'"(Matthew 9:36-38)*

If I am going to seek to emulate Jesus, one of the first things that needs to change in me is my eyesight. The reason I say that is because so often when I see people in the everyday business of life it doesn't cross my mind that they might be 'harassed and helpless'. If God helps me to see other humans as He sees them, in need of a Shepherd, this would change my approach. Added to this, it would also change my emotional response; I would 'have compassion'. This phrase means that Jesus felt a gut wrenching ache as he saw how lost these people were. Compassion was the main engine which drove Jesus in his earthly ministry, even to the point of crucifixion.

The final insight I have from this incident is the result of the disciples being asked by the Lord to pray for workers in the harvest of souls. As I'm sure you know, when these words were originally written there were no chapter divisions. So going forwards into chapter ten, Matthew tells us the names of the disciples, but the next words of significance are

"…These twelve Jesus sent out…" (Matthew 10:5)

Those praying became the workers, the harvesters! So very often we are the answer to our own prayers. Of course it's really imperative that we pray for lost people, but if we don't do something with our prayers we may be guilty of only doing half of the job. Is there some person or situation you have been praying about? Ask yourself whether there is anything you can do in cooperation with God to bring about an answer to the prayers you have been praying.

The second Scripture which God has used to move me forwards evangelistically is this:

"For we must all appear before the judgment seat of Christ, so that each of us may receive what is due to us for the things done while in the body, whether good or bad.

Since, then, we know what it is to fear the Lord, we try to persuade others. What we are is plain to God, and I hope it is also plain to your conscience. We are not trying to commend ourselves to you again, but are giving you an opportunity to take pride in us, so that you can answer those who take pride in what is seen rather than in what is in the heart. If we are 'out of our mind,' as some say, it is for God; if we are in our right mind, it is for you. For Christ's love compels us, because we are convinced that one died for all, and therefore all died. And he died for all, that those who live should no longer live for themselves but for him who died for them and was raised again.

So from now on we regard no one from a worldly point of view. Though we once regarded Christ in this way, we do so no longer. Therefore, if anyone is in Christ, the new creation has come: the old has gone, the new is here! All this is from God, who reconciled us to himself through Christ and gave us the ministry of reconciliation: that God was reconciling the world to himself in Christ,

60

> *not counting people's sins against them. And he has*
> *committed to us the message of reconciliation. We are*
> *therefore Christ's ambassadors, as though God were*
> *making his appeal through us. We implore you on*
> *Christ's behalf: be reconciled to God. God made him*
> *who had no sin to be sin for us, so that in him we might*
> *become the righteousness of God."*
> *(2 Corinthians 5:10-20)*

What a challenge! First of all, Paul reminds us that there will be an evaluation in terms of how we have behaved and also whether we have sought to share the Gospel with others (vv10, 11). Is it possible for there to be any sense of Jesus being disappointed with us when we meet him face to face? I'm not sure there is, but in the light of all he's done for me I want to live and speak as an authentic disciple while I am still here on Earth.

Then, Paul writes about how the love of Christ is the motivating factor for us in evangelism. This works on two levels. To start, if we have a clear revelation that Jesus gave everything he had for us on the cross as a demonstration of his love, then it makes complete sense that I would be compelled to share that message with others. In one translation of this passage it reads 'the love of Christ leaves us no choice...' Or does it?

At the end of the chapter, the Apostle reminds us that we are not merely those who made an historical decision to trust in Jesus: right here and right now we are Christ's ambassadors, speaking up for our King and His Kingdom, inviting others to cross over from the realm of darkness into His wonderful, bright, Kingdom! Notice the sense of passion and emotion in the words 'we implore you' (v19). We are not asking someone merely to give an intellectual assent to the Gospel; this is an invitation to enter a whole new way of living!

So, we have the passion, but what about the practicalities? How do we as disciples of Jesus help others to find him?

For Reflection/Discussion

1. Out of the five common issues that put a 'brake' on our evangelistic witness, which would be the top two for you personally?

2. What needs to happen in the next few months to help you overcome the inertia you have in these two areas?

3. Of the motivational factors mentioned in the Bible passages, how many particularly resonated with you? Why?

DISCIPLESHIP: HELPING SOMEONE ON THE JOURNEY TO FAITH
Disciple-Making Precedes Salvation

It's often the case that a person has begun the journey towards God before they have had any meaningful interaction with a fully-fledged disciple of Jesus. For example, the person may have concluded that God is real through observing the wonders of creation (Psalm 19:1-4). The apostle Paul goes even further, asserting that no one has any excuse for unbelief:

> *"For since the creation of the world God's invisible qualities – his eternal power and divine nature – have been clearly seen, being understood from what has been made, so that people are without excuse."*
> *(Romans 1:20)*

It could be that this person has watched a brilliant sunset or marvelled at the intricacies of a spiders web or been blown away at the beauty of a new born child: there is thankfulness, but to whom?

And then comes the day when he/she meets you. It could be a new job, a house move, a sports team or any number of other ways this happens. Let's take it for granted that you are doing your best, with God's help, to follow Jesus. How can you be a spiritual catalyst in this person's journey?

Here are seven things to do to help someone come to faith:

• Pray for them

Guess what? God answers our prayers! You have probably heard the teaching that His answer can be yes, no or wait. But if you are praying for someone you know to move along the discipleship continuum, I believe God answers in the affirmative! Now you might wonder then why the person you are praying for has not already made any great or obvious spiritual move. Even though God is not willing that any should perish (2 Peter 3:9), His will can be thwarted through a person's will and/or even satanic deception. But keep praying! Circumstances can turn around in a moment. Think of Saul on the Damascus Road '...breathing out murderous threats against the Lord's disciples...' (Acts 9:1) just before he meets Jesus!

One thing of which I'm sure: it's rare if ever that someone comes to the point of salvation unless someone somewhere has been praying for them. How prayer works is a mystery in many ways, but we know that far, far more happens when we pray than if we don't really bother.

• Share Your Life

Even if you discount the work of the Holy Spirit (!!), the law of averages suggests that the more you hang out with someone and build a strong friendship, the more chance there is of discussing the deeper things of life including faith, purpose, identity, etc.

No doubt there are people you know who are not Jesus followers; but how much do you 'know' them? Are they more than simply an acquaintance? In the busyness of life it's not possible to get to build deep friendships with lots of people at the same time so you are going to have to approach this with a cool head, a warm heart and listening for the 'nudge' from God. So begin to ask the Lord "who should I try and get to know better?" Often your common sense will be a strong guide. The most obvious persons will be those who are similar to you in terms of age, interests, family life or sense of humour. It also helps if you have plenty of potential opportunities to be together, so work colleagues, family or neighbours fit well.

Now you might be thinking that this approach is all a bit clinical. I can understand that, but as has been said so often, if you aim at nothing, guess what you hit? And if you simply rely on things happening accidently, it rarely works. The 'scattergun' approach to evangelism means we produce lots of output but probably little outcome. Better to reach one by one than risk reaching no one in an effective manner. Let me remind you that we are aiming at making disciples so if we can reach, equip and release just one person at a time into the human harvest field we are, over time, potentially looking at exponentially increasing the number of Jesus followers. Added to this, if you truly care about someone, you will want the best for them. Well, what is the best you could want for anyone? Proactively seeking to reach someone for Christ is an act of love.

• Share Your Story

One of the main ways in which the dragon, Satan is defeated is through '...the word of their [our] testimony...' (Revelation 12:11). If we can take opportunities to share with our friends the difference that following Jesus has made in our lives, God will use this powerfully. He may use what we say to remove the spiritual blindness which the devil often places over the minds of human beings (2 Corinthians 4:4).

Actually, you have more than one story to tell. How you came to a saving knowledge of Christ is of course foundational, but what about all the other times when the Lord has intervened in a positive way in your life? The most powerful witness is when you can link what is happening in a friend's situation to something very similar that you have experienced. For example, what about if someone is going through a time of rejection? Maybe they have lost their job, a boy/girlfriend has finished the relationship or, God forbid, a spouse has cheated on them. If you have suffered something very close to their experience and you found great help and support from Jesus, then share it in a gentle and respectful way.

• Share your Friends

It can be really helpful for an unbelieving friend to discover that there are lots more people like you in the world! It's not so much that your friend needs to be preached at by another Christian! Rather, there is something about the atmosphere of being with a gaggle of disciples which can have a profound impact. The life, love, joy, kindness and unity speaks volumes. The early church father, Tertullian pointed out in the 2nd century AD that Christians were known for how they loved one another.[8]

---

[8] Tertullian, *Apologeticus pro Christianis*, ch39.

I remember a young man called Jamie who came to faith. The main motivating factor for him was experiencing the house group which he'd been invited to join. He told me that it felt like a loving family and he wanted to be part of it. The key he realised was to have God as his Father!

Do you feel as if you don't really have time to get involved in reaching out to lost people? In the main it's simply about including them in on what you are already doing with your believing friends. Cinema? Restaurant? Gym? Holiday? Even church!! You can always invite them along.

• Invite to Alpha?

Globally, more than twenty million people have graduated from the Alpha Course. There are so many variations available now so that it can be run in all kinds of contexts: a church building, a living room or even online through a Zoom group or some other social media networking tool.

Taking a friend along means you get to eat together, talk about questions or objections to faith and, in a non-coercive environment, there is opportunity for someone to cross over into a living friendship with their Creator!

There are other 'process evangelism' courses available and it is possible to put together a series of meetings for a group of friends which is particularly tailored to their questions or needs, but I have found the Alpha Course to be the most accessible ready-made course out there.

• "Read this!"

Some people process things through thinking and others more through feelings. If your friend is primarily a thinker, give them something to read which will challenge them to evaluate or re-evaluate what they believe. There are so many good quality publications on the market today which aim to show the coherence and credibility of Christianity to those who have deep questions. If you are interested to find something and you're not sure where to look, ask a church leader for help!

• You're Invited!

If your friend is someone who processes more subjectively, meaning they are a 'feeler', why not do something radical and invite them to church! Obviously you need to use your sanctified common sense in terms of which church and what kind of church service you invite them to! For some seekers the sense of awe during worship and the passionate preaching of God's truth opens their hearts up to receiving the free gift of salvation or it moves them ever closer to that glorious moment!

• Stay friends

This final step is all-important. What will you do if your friend decides that they are really not interested or not willing to pursue discipleship? Is that the end of your friendship? If so, it's clear that you have not acted in a godly fashion. This person was simply 'conversion fodder' rather than someone to be loved just as they are irrespective of any decision they might make.

> *"If it is possible, as far as it depends on you, live at peace with everyone." (Romans 12:18)*

In reality, some friendships last a lifetime and others seem to be more for a season. But if there is a deliberate pulling away from friendship, let it be from them, not from you!

So often, someone says 'no' to God at one time and then years later makes a decision to follow Christ. My good friend Mark Greenwood wrote an excellent book on the evangelistic process called *Big Yes, Little Yes, Healthy Maybe.*[9] In this chapter I have laid out in a kind of timeline the steps by which someone might come to the point of trusting Jesus for initial salvation. Mark's book has lots more to say about this. But in reality things rarely run smoothly: there are ups and downs in the journey. Just when you think a person is about to say a 'Big Yes', they totally back off. Hang in there if you possibly can. It's not over until it's over! Discipling someone through to the point of salvation rarely runs smoothly.

---

[9] M. Greenwood, *Big Yes Little Yes Healthy Maybe* (VeriteCM, 2019).

For Reflection/Discussion

1. In an attitude of prayer, think about those you know who do not follow Jesus. Name three who you sense you could begin to disciple towards salvation. What are their names?

2. Where would you place each of them on the 'Big Yes, Little Yes, Healthy Maybe' scale?

3. Work through the 'steps to take' and begin to imagine and plan what you might be able to do to facilitate your friends moving towards Jesus.

DISCIPLESHIP: EXAMINING THE SPIRITUAL PATHWAY

Moving From Death to Life to Growth

It may well be a spoof story or 'fake news' as it is more often called these days, but there was a ridiculously silly post going around recently which goes as follows...

A zoo in Cairo had no zebras. Zebras aren't indigenous to Egypt and visitors to the zoo wanted to see some. The zoo came up with a cunning plan. Rather than buy zebras from another zoo and import them, they decided to paint black and white stripes on two donkeys which already lived at the zoo.

Now this raises all sorts of questions in my mind. First of all, how did the painters manage to get the donkeys to remain still while they applied the stripes? Second, what happens when the paint wears off? And another thing; where is the integrity?

Now, if you were an Egyptian living in Cairo and you had never seen a zebra up close, it's possible that you could be fooled for a while. But sooner or later the truth will out.

There is always the danger that, when it comes to discipleship, we can end up with painted donkeys rather than the real thing. You see, to be an ongoing disciple of Jesus must mean that something has been transformed in our spiritual DNA. If ever we think that being a true follower is simply to do with outward conformity to some clear moral principles then we are no more necessarily Christian than a good atheist, or Buddhist or... (fill in the gap yourself!).

It's important at this point that you don't misunderstand me on two particular issues.

The first is, as has been alluded to, that the discipleship journey usually begins before the experience and reality of salvation kicks in. On an individual level it may not be recognised at the time, but

God is at work in someone's life long before they are consciously aware of the fact.

Secondly, over a period of time, the evidence of salvation will be seen in a changed life. Some commentators will suggest that it is possible to be a Christian without much or any moral/spiritual transformation having taken place. It's the other side, the antithesis of the donkey/zebra illustration. It means that we can be a lying, cheating, violent, drunken serial adulterer, but because we prayed 'the sinners prayer' way back in the day, we have our 'fire insurance' in place for when we die. Can I beg to differ?

Even before Jesus came on the scene in his public ministry, his cousin John was telling the religious people to '...produce fruit in keeping with repentance...' (Matthew 3:8). Later on, Jesus's brother writing about those who failed to care for those less fortunate declared:

> *"You see that a person is justified [put right with God]
> by what he does and not by faith alone."(James 2:24)*

What both John the Baptist and James were pointing out was that saving faith in Jesus is evidenced by how you live your life. This will become clearer, I hope, as we unpack the discipleship pathway below.

The Pathway to Birth – My Journey

C.S. Lewis, the author of the Narnia books once wrote

> *"Agnostics talk cheerfully of man's search for God
> but they might as well talk about the mouse's search
> for the cat."[10]*

In other words, God is after each one of us!

As a seventeen year old young man who had no overt Christian background, I came to a living faith in May, 1974. Even so, I can see

---

[10] C.S. Lewis, *Surprised by Joy* (Collins, 2012).

in retrospect that there were several steps where it seems God was reaching out to me with his loving presence before the penny dropped.

For a couple of years at school I had an excellent RE teacher, Mr Harris (I still find it difficult to refer to him now as 'George'). He taught us about all religions, but seemed to come alive when he spoke about Jesus. I discovered many years later that he prayed for his students regularly in his devotions. He invited us to a youth club at his Baptist church and a bunch of us went over regularly, mainly to the discos because the young women there were particularly pretty. Through all of this, something was going in! Whether it was the gracious way I was treated by the youth leaders or some truth about Jesus which got lodged in my brain during conversations, the seed of the Gospel was being sown into me.

On another occasion, I remember coming back from the pub late one night, worse for wear. I switched on the TV and heard a man describing his best friend who sounded incredible, someone I'd like to know. At the end of the broadcast he announced that his friend's name was Jesus. What I hadn't realised was that I had been watching the Epilogue which in those days was usually the last programme before broadcasting finished for the day. I was shocked, but also intrigued to find out more about this Jesus, but by the next morning I had forgotten all about it. Or so I thought!

Then there was the school Christmas carol service, held on Wednesday afternoon replacing double maths – hallelujah! I was sitting in the middle of around four hundred other students as a trendy vicar spoke about the difference Jesus had made in his life. Halfway through he pointed directly at me and asked me to help him with a question. A four hundred to one chance! I was impressed by what he had shared and wanted to go to the coffee bar they were running at the local church to find out more, but none of my mates were interested so peer pressure won the day.

Five months later and I was on a geography field course in Snowdonia and ended up sitting next to a minister's daughter for dinner every evening. She had said a 'Big Yes' to following Jesus at the Christmas coffee bar that I hadn't gone to, and was happy to answer my questions about faith. Unknown to me, she called home and made sure many folks in her church were praying for me. When we arrived back after the course her dad, Tom Hall (remember him from earlier in the book?) introduced himself to me and offered his help if I had any further questions. Right there and then I asked him if he could spare some time. Two hours later, in his study at the manse (vicarage), I knelt down and welcomed Jesus into my life.

It was for me a 'Damascus Road' experience. I had been 'born again' (John 3:3). But there was a whole backstory where God had been calling me to follow Jesus even though I didn't fully recognise it at the time.

The Pathway to Birth - Peter's Journey

Here's an intriguing question: when was the Apostle Peter saved? It seems from the Gospel accounts that he had met Jesus before he was called to follow and fish for people (look at John 1:35-42 and then Luke 5:1-11). So it's clear that he had become a follower, a disciple, but was Peter saved at this point?

Perhaps it was when he had the revelation of who Jesus really was (Matthew 16:16), although within a sentence or two he is rebuking the Lord who then called him Satan. Or maybe it was on the Mount of Transfiguration when he sees Jesus in all his glory (Matthew 17:1-8)? Perhaps when the resurrected Lord restores him (John 21:15-22)?

The fact of the matter is that we don't know for sure when Peter was truly saved, but we know at some point, he was!

The reason why I shared my story and Peter's story is to make the point that often we use the terms 'discipleship' and 'evangelism' in a binary way without recognising that there may be overlap between the two.

Now, from God's perspective, there is definitely a moment in time when someone is saved, born again, regenerated, receives the gift of eternal life or whatever terminology you might use. Paul makes this clear here:

> *"As for you, you were dead in your transgressions and sins, in which you used to live when you followed the ways of this world and of the ruler of the kingdom of the air, the spirit who is now at work in those who are disobedient...But because of his great love for us, God, who is rich in mercy, made us alive with Christ even when we were dead in transgressions—it is by grace you have been saved." (Ephesians 2:1,2,4,5)*

Many Jesus followers are not sure when this crisis moment happened for them: others know the exact moment. But as someone has pointed out, it's not knowing when you were born that is critically important; it's knowing that you are alive!

Back in 1991, the Berlin Wall had only come down a short while before and the former Eastern European nations were still in a state of confusion and turmoil. I led a team which consisted of a gospel rock band, a young evangelist and myself. We set off in our van to play some gigs in Estonia. The journey was quite an adventure, driving pretty much non-stop through nine countries with a few detours thrown in! As we passed through borders, the driver and navigator knew for sure that we were now in a different nation. The rest of the crew were asleep in the back of the van and were unaware. Even so, they also had crossed over but it only dawned on them later as they woke up and noticed the new terrain or language or food. Spiritually, a similar thing takes place.

The point is that 'followership' begins for many even before they have crossed over into eternal life with Christ. They may be heading for the initial 'salvation border' and even cross over without at first realising what has happened. For many, it's only in retrospect that they know for sure that everything has changed.

Nurturing the Baby

In order for spiritual initiation to take place so that someone becomes a fruitful child of God, there has to be a point in the process when one chooses to take several deliberate steps. These are:

- **Repentance towards God.** This involves a turning away from doing our own thing and a turning back to God in order to receive the gift of eternal life.

- **Faith in the Lord Jesus** and what he has done. Faith is a gift and the Lord gives it freely to anyone who truly comes to Him. A person is given the ability to trust in all that was done for him/her through the death and resurrection of Christ.

- **Baptism in water.** Forgive me if this is a difficult thing to grasp, but personally I can find no evidence in the Bible to suggest that baptism was experienced by any person unless they had decided to follow Jesus.

- **Baptism (filling) with the Holy Spirit.** It's possible to be forgiven without being filled, to be saved without being saturated with God's presence, power and Person!

Please notice that here we are addressing the total package of initiation. As is often pointed out, the thief on the cross next to Jesus was promised Paradise without being baptised in water or the Spirit, but for the rest of us who are not going to die within the next hour or two (!!) there is a pathway of obedience (baptism) and blessing (filling) which sets us up for a strong walk with God into our destiny.[11]

Dr William Abraham[12] would want to take this nurture period even further and believes that for someone to be fully initiated into the Kingdom of God, a belief in the early church creeds is imperative as

---

[11] D. Pawson. *The Normal Christian Birth* (Hodder & Stoughton, 1997).

[12] W.J. Abraham. *The Logic of Evangelism* (Hodder & Stoughton, 1989).

well as the reception and use of spiritual gifts. For me this is a clear illustration of how the discipleship/evangelism continuum overlap. We have here the dichotomy between what God sees and knows about someone's spiritual state and their future trajectory versus the little we know as disciple makers about these issues. The simple point to make is that whatever point the new disciple is at, our job is to help this person to mature in Christ.

In the early church a new disciple might spend up to three years undergoing catechesis (nurturing discipleship) before being fully absorbed into the church family[13]. There may have been particular reasons for this: for example the concern of the church leaders that they were not being infiltrated by those who were seeking to destroy the church. Also many of the new converts were from pagan rather than Jewish backgrounds and therefore needed a more extensive reorientation of their worldview. Maybe there was also the thought that the first disciples went through three years of what we might term catechesis with Jesus before the Church was born and so this was a model? (This is a personal thought and may be way off!).

The model of the early church is different to our approach today. This in itself is not wrong given that we live in a world with its own cultural distinctives. The way it was done in the first few hundred years of the Church is what we might term 'descriptive' rather than 'prescriptive', but the basic principle of a processed initiation into following Jesus still holds good.

In our day the Church has mainly opted for approaches which might be seen as a 'mini-catechesis' for those who are on a path to being fully fledged disciples. Previously I wrote about The Alpha Course as a means of helping a friend come to saving faith. However, the mixture of sessions covers not only Gospel explanation but also the basics of Christian living and has proved highly effective in facilitating the early stages of discipleship growth. One of the

---

[13] C.E. Arnold. *"Early Church Catechesis and New Christians' Classes in Contemporary Evangelicalism"* (JETS 47/1, March 2004). Sourced from https://www.etsjets.org/files/JETS-PDFs/47/47-1/47-1-pp039-054_JETS.pdf

great benefits of the Course is its appeal to the intellect as well as the emotional/spiritual aspect of friendship with God. Participants are given something like ten or eleven weeks in a non-coercive atmosphere to decide whether they truly wish to follow Jesus. The result for many is that any commitment is more profound and less 'flash in the pan' in nature. Added to this, the context for working things through is a small group dynamic which, as we shall discover, is one strong key for effective discipleship.

Growing Up

So now we have a young spiritual child on our hands or even a nursery full of them (Please, God!). How do we continue the nurturing in order to produce strong believers who are able to stand? For me, it's important to engage the whole person in the process, something which has been described as 'Head: Heart: Hands.'

• Head

Loving God with our mind is part of what we are called to do based on the Great Command (Matthew 22:37). This does not require that we all become theological academics, but it does mean that we learn the basis for our faith from the scriptures.

Every person chooses deliberately or by default where they look for the authority to govern how they live and behave. Most people simply rely on what others have told them or on what they think or feel from their own perspective. A disciple of Jesus looks to the Bible for their plumb line in what they believe and how they therefore live their life. Jesus said error comes if we '...don't know the scriptures or the power of God...' (Mark 12:24). Added to this, Paul advises his spiritual son Timothy:

> *"Do your best to present yourself to God as one*
> *approved, a worker who does not need to be ashamed*
> *and who correctly handles the word of truth."*
> *(2 Tim 2:15)*

It's not possible to categorically prove to someone else that the Bible is the Creator's manual for how best to live and thrive in this life, but the experience of millions of Jesus followers through the centuries has been that when they have entrusted the Scriptures to show them who the Lord is and how to follow in His ways they have been blessed, helped and guided, sometimes in remarkable ways.

There is an inherent danger of course in making a certain passage of scripture mean whatever we want it to mean in order that we can simply do what we want to do anyway. So it's critical that we know how the Bible holds together, what it teaches and how to interpret it correctly[14]. Now God can very occasionally change the rules in order to speak into a very specific situation in your life, and he does, but this is the exception not the rule! It's also the reason why he has placed us in community, the local church, so that on those rare occasions when Scripture seems to be leading us in a specific direction, others can 'weigh it' with us. More on this, with some personal examples when we look at being discipled through the agency of Scripture.

Some years back, in my local church, we experienced a lot of new people deciding to surrender to King Jesus, mainly as a result of attending the Alpha Course. What next? I decided to write a short nurture course for new believers called 'Walking with Jesus' which seemed to do the job and was published shortly afterwards by a national ministry. Recently as I re-read it, I realised that it was now out of date because the use of language had changed in ten years and helps such as Bible apps were now available. So it is now rewritten and republished as 'The Walk'[15]. It aims to deal with twelve of the major areas of Christian living based on what the Bible teaches. Rather than deal with it here, I have included a copy of the course at the back of the book together with an explanation of the philosophy behind its compilation. 'The Walk' has now been road

---

[14] G.D. Fee & D. Stuart. *How to Read the Bible for all its Worth* (Zondervan, 2014).

[15] G. Gibbs. *The Walk. Becoming a Jesus Follower* (Self-published, 2019).

tested with many new Jesus followers and over more than a decade, so even though this is a self-commendation, I'd like to recommend it as a way of putting strong biblical foundations into a young believer.

• Heart

There is something deep within the psyche of human beings which means we must worship. Everyone worships something, whether it be a sports team, a particular hobby, money, another person or simply themselves! I believe the reason behind this is to do with the way we were created. In 1647, the Westminster Shorter Catechism declared that:

> *"Man's chief end is to glorify God, and to enjoy him for ever."*[16]

It is often wonderfully emotive when we turn towards God expressing our love and adoration to Him. Of course, worship is more than singing or praying; our whole lives are supposed to be an act of worship, but it is the case that whether alone or joining with others in telling the Lord how much we honour and love Him can often be a moving occasion.

Having said that, in Scripture, the heart is not simply where our feelings are based. Rather, it is seen as the very centre of who we are as person. So to love God with all our heart means that we offer up all that we have and are to Him. That's why this third area of engagement is so relevant...

• Hands

Our bodies are to honour God (1 Corinthians 6:20). We are literally to be 'do-gooders'! The engine which drives us out to serve the world around us is our faith in Jesus. Church history is full of stories of believers who have done heroic and sacrificial exploits simply because they loved God and the people He had made. If I mention

---

[16] P. Rollinson & D.F. Kelly. *The Westminster Shorter Catechism in Modern English* (P&R Publishing, 1990).

organisations which exist today such as Barnardo's, Leprosy Mission, Christian Aid, Tear Fund, World Vision, RSPCA, Christians Against Poverty, Trussell Trust food banks, etc., all of them had or still have Christian roots. In the 19th Century it was the persistence of William Wilberforce which eventually led to the abolition of the slave trade. Lord Shaftesbury stopped little children being used in child labour. And we could go on.

On an individual level, every disciple is called to love his/her neighbour as him/herself (Matthew 22:39). So it's imperative for us to learn to live unselfish lives where we practically care for the needs of those around us and across the world. We do so in a way which may cost us in terms of time, money and energy. There is hardly a day that goes by when you and I are not provided with an opportunity to manifest the kindness of God to our neighbours, family, work colleagues or some random stranger.

Peter preached that Jesus in his earthly life '...went about doing good...' (Acts 10:38). That is a major part of our calling too! It's rare to find a local church which is not involved in serving its community through social action projects relevant to the local area. As a functioning Jesus follower there are great opportunities to demonstrate the love of God in very practical ways, serving alongside other believers.

For Reflection/Discussion

1. Can you recognise some steps or experiences which preceded your conversion but were part of the journey? What were they?

2. Have you experienced the four steps of initiation into the Kingdom of God mentioned in this chapter? If not, why haven't these things happened? Lack of opportunity? Unaware? Some other reason?

3. We grow as believers when we engage 'Head, Heart, Hands.' Which of these three areas do you find least difficult? How would you strengthen the other two?

DISCIPLESHIP: THE PATHWAY TO MATURITY
Co-operating with God in Our Growth

I still remember when our eldest child, Ben was born. It was a bit traumatic because the medics decided to perform an emergency Caesarean section. As a result, Sally was still being treated in the operating theatre when Ben was brought to me, wrapped in a white cloth. The nurse who brought him to me said "Well! Look at him! He's just like his dad!" Now at that moment, Ben's face was all scrunched up with lots of skin folds. He was completely toothless. He was squinting through barely open eyes. And the nurse thought he looked like me! Cheeky woman! As I write, all these years later, something remarkable has taken place. Benjamin James Gibbs looks like a younger, slimmer version of his dad!

The point is simply this: we are to grow in godliness, to become more like our Heavenly Dad.

The New Testament is clear that God's desire for each of us is that we do not remain as spiritual children, needing constant care and attention in an unhealthily dependent way. The Lord wants us to move on to maturity, that we become more Christ-like. In this way we will look just like our Dad or our elder Brother!

Here are just a handful of encouragements and motivations towards growth:

- Keep pressing on to the goal (maturity)! Philippians 3:13-15

- Grow up and take solid food (God's word), not milk! Hebrews 5:11-13

- Endure hardship as discipline! Hebrews 12:7

- Persevere to become mature! James 1:4

The question then is "what are the tools we need to move on and develop?"

Spiritual Fruit

But the fruit of the Spirit is love, joy, peace, patience, kindness, goodness, faithfulness, gentleness and self-control. (Galatians 5:22)

I'm not a gardener and the back of our home doesn't have lots of space. Even so, Sally has been growing some fruit, namely rhubarb and raspberries. I have the job of watering everything when it's warm and we haven't had any rain for quite a few days. The good news is that I haven't killed off the fruit. The bad news is that it seems to take forever to grow to the point when it's edible! Already the rhubarb looks like rhubarb, except its very small, and the raspberries are tiny little green things, but I can tell what they will become in a month or two. Fruit takes time to grow to maturity and it will only do so if it is watered and fed.

When I made the initial decision to follow Jesus, some things changed overnight. Previously I had what some might call a 'potty mouth', but the day after experiencing the forgiveness and love of Christ, I discovered I wasn't swearing anymore. I sometimes joke that I lost half of my vocabulary at that point! Also, my desire to get drunk on a fairly regular basis disappeared. Imagine my excitement the first time I opened a Bible, not knowing where to begin, so randomly flicking it open and reading the first sentence I looked at:

Therefore, if anyone is in Christ, the new creation has come: the old has gone, the new is here! All this is from God, who reconciled us to himself through Christ... (2 Corinthians 5:17, 18)

So a tiny amount of the fruit of the Spirit was already being evidenced in my new life, namely self-control. Now, more than forty six years later, I have to confess that I am still very much a 'work in progress'. In fact, I feel that way more than ever!

How does the fruit of the Spirit grow in our lives?

It's pretty obvious that a person does not have to be a Jesus follower to exhibit the characteristics outlined in Galatians 5:22. I have atheist friends, some of whom show these markers more than some of my believing friends! So what is going on? Well, every human being is created in the image of God and even though, as we have seen, the image is distorted due to the transmission of sinfulness, the ruinous effects have not completely removed the image. Moreover, the original image can be more intact in some lives than others depending on factors such as upbringing, temperament, strength of character, motivations, etc.

When someone welcomes the Holy Spirit of Jesus into their life, the potential for these desired character qualities to grow is supernaturally enhanced above and beyond what would normally be the case. It is true however that some begin far further back morally than others and so the evaluation of a changed life in someone who claims Christ as Lord depends on what the state of their life was when they started out on this journey.

Let's also be clear on another issue. The growth of these qualities is not automatic in the life of a professed Christian. We all know of church people who are unloving, lemon-faced, impatient, unkind, and vicious. Of course this begs the question as to whether they have ever truly encountered the transforming power of the Holy Spirit or have embraced a discipleship journey of any consequence. A genuine Jesus follower will be one who chooses to partner with God in desiring the fruit to grow. It requires a surrendering of the human will to the will of God. As we choose partnership and surrender, then in the 'stuff of life' the fruit has opportunity to mature. For instance, how will patience develop unless there is a situation which has the potential for impatience? Or, how will we learn to be gentle unless there is an occasion when we are tempted to be harsh?

The fruit of the Spirit make us grow to be more like Jesus temperamentally and in how we positively and unselfishly engage with other people. There is a word for what is being described here; Sanctification. Delicatessen is another big word but nowhere near as important!

I was just about to finish writing for today when this quote popped up on my social media:

> *"Your greatest test will be how you handle people who mishandle you."*

It's in exactly these tests that the fruit of the Spirit is manifested and formed. Our character is revealed not so much in our actions as in our reactions!

On a practical level it's not difficult to see that the context in which the fruit can grow is when we are doing life with others. The two places where most of us spend most of our time are the workplace and the home and so inevitably these will be where we have opportunity to either grow in our Christlikeness or to be spiritual imposters: let's choose growth.

Spiritual Gifts

Fruit grows by a process over time. Gifts on the other hand, come instantly, but still need to be worked on and enhanced. For example, a couple of my grandsons (I've got five up until now) really like Lego. Choosing gifts for birthdays and Christmas is easy! But what would be the point of the boys receiving their presents and simply leaving them in the boxes? Of course what they do is unwrap the bricks and build some amazing buildings, vehicles and other contraptions with the pieces.

You and I have natural gifts given to us by our Creator even before we are born. Sometimes these gifts never come to their full potential and that is sad. We also receive gifts from the Lord once we are saved and filled with His Spirit. How sad it is when believers fail to receive these gifts and/or fail to develop the gifts to their fullest extent.

Some parts of the Church recognise that God has offered nine gifts of the Holy Spirit, all of which are mentioned in 1 Corinthians 12:7-11. No doubt these are significant as we shall see, but it can be argued that there are at least 28 spiritual gifts mentioned in the New Testament and even then this may not be an exhaustive list.

Back in 1979, C. Peter Wagner wrote a book entitled *Your Spiritual Gifts Can Help Your Church Grow*[17]. (updated in 2012). Many of us 'oldies' have benefitted from what he wrote, but at the time the focus of much of the Church was mainly around the issue of church growth, meaning numbers. Into the 1990s and Rick Warren insightfully made the point that the fundamental issue is not church growth but rather church health[18]. The church is the Body of Christ and healthy bodies grow! Quite simply, if disciples discover their spiritual gifts and use them, there will be results!

If for a moment we focus in on the list of nine gifts, or manifestations in 1 Corinthians12 we discover something which I think is really illuminating. Reading through the list, ask yourself, which gifts did Jesus of Nazareth have or operate in? (At this point, you may need to open a Bible!). It doesn't take much thinking to recognise that he used at least seven. It's not possible to say whether he prayed in private using the gift of tongues and of course the gift of interpretation wasn't necessary until the Church was born at Pentecost. The reason why this is important is because, as we have seen, God has destined us to become like Jesus (Romans 8:29). Added to this, John writes:

> *... whoever claims to live in him must live as Jesus did.*
> *(1John 2:6)*

Often we limit what God can do with us and through us because we think that He only gives each person one gift unless on a particular day He is feeling extra generous! But if this is the case how can I be like Jesus in terms of giftedness if at best I only receive a seventh of the gifts he had in his earthly ministry? Actually, even more so, if we look at the twenty eight gifts identified by Wagner, Jesus operated in nearly all of them at some point.

---

[17] C.P. Wagner. *Your Spiritual Gifts Can Help Your Church Grow* (Chosen Books, 2012).

[18] R. Warren. *The Purpose Driven Church* (Zondervan, 1996).

Another way of looking at this is to view the gifts as 'manifestations' (1 Corinthians 12:7). From this perspective, since the Manifester (the Holy Spirit) lives in me, He can manifest Himself through me at a particular time for a particular purpose. So, for example, if someone has a broken wrist, a word of knowledge is not much use ("I perceive you are in pain in the lower arm area!"). What would be much more helpful would be a gift of healing!

The conclusion is that from a biblical perspective, our generous God will gift us in multiple ways. In present day reality we know this is the case since the majority of Jesus followers are multi-gifted.

What are gifts for? Well, if the fruit of the Spirit make us morally like Jesus, spiritual gifts enable us to do the works of Jesus particularly in the missional arena. These gifts are a toolbox through which the Kingly rule of Jesus can be manifested through his Church. This becomes obvious through the book of Acts where we discover all sorts of spiritual gifts being used as the Gospel is planted into towns and cities and the Church begins.

The gifts are not for us to show off and display our supernatural credentials; neither are they a mark of spiritual maturity. Any of us who have been on this journey with Jesus for a long time will know of people who were amazingly gifted by God and fell for the deception that it was something intrinsic in them which enabled them to do signs, miracles or wonders. Some of these same people are no longer walking with the Lord or they have ended up disillusioned and disappointed. That is why the combination of developing the fruit of the Spirit alongside these functional gifts from the Spirit is so powerful. It's like the two wings of a bird; if we only have one wing we go round and round in circles, but with two we can really fly and get somewhere!

How should we go about receiving spiritual gifts? Or how should we discover and develop whatever spiritual gifts we already have? Here are some thoughts:

- Paul writes that we should 'earnestly desire spiritual gifts' (1 Corinthians 14:1). Similarly, Jesus taught us to ask for good gifts (Matthew 7:7-11). In other words, what would you like to do for Jesus and what gifts would you need? Ask Him!

- Ask with the right attitude (James 4:3). A desire to glorify God, to bless others and to share the Gospel in power are preferred motivations.

- Ask trusted believing friends to help you work out what gifts you have, even if at this stage they are embryonic. Don't simply ask those who will agree with whatever you say!

- Do a spiritual gifts inventory such as the one in Wagner's book.

- Find a mature Jesus follower who already has these same kind of gifts and ask them to help you develop in these areas.

- Use the gift(s)! If you do so under supervision of leaders who love you and want you to be useful to the Lord, the gifts will develop.

- Don't forget that practice makes permanent, not perfect! A golfer can practice his/her swing for hours on end, but if the grip is wrong or how they stand when addressing the golf ball is incorrect they will simply become permanently bad at hitting a shot. At the very least, they will need intensive coaching to correct the mistakes. Similarly, if you use the gifts in a selfish way with a motivation to make you look good in other people's eyes, it will eventually stick. So make sure your practice is undergirded by a sincere love for people and a desire for God's glory, not yours!

For Reflection/Discussion

1. Read through the list of the fruit of the Spirit (Galatians 5:22, 23). Which two or three need to be given particular attention for you? How will you cooperate with God on these?

2. Which spiritual gifts do you recognise in your own life? (If you're not sure, ask a few trusted Christian friends!). Can you think of particular contexts where these might be used?

3. Which spiritual gifts would you like to experience being manifested through you more regularly? How might this happen?

4. What is your greatest fear about growing in Christlikeness?

DISCIPLESHIP BY THE WORD AND THE SPIRIT

God's Agents for Growth

As we have seen, God often uses human agents to bring about transformation in our lives.

I remember many years ago arriving at a 'welcome meeting' with a church. We were due to spend a couple of weeks helping them with their outreach. At the end of the evening a smallish man wearing glasses came up to me and asked if I would like to have a free golf lesson sometime over the next few days. I mumbled something about not being sure what my itinerary was, but I'd get back to him if it were possible. I later discovered that this man coached some of the top golfers in the world! Later that week after no more than fifty minutes with the coach, I was hitting the ball as sweet as a nut - and straight as well!

There are a number of stories I could tell where the Lord has used people with greater skill and godliness than I will ever possess to adjust my life trajectory is some positive way. But what about if you and a bunch of people who were not Jesus followers were washed up on a proverbial desert island and you had nothing with you except for a Bible. How would discipleship work then? How would you grow in your ministry and the mission before you?

Whether it is the highly unlikely scenario described above or the situation we face in the real world, the Word of God and the Spirit of God are crucial keys if we are to grow in Christlikeness.

As you may be aware, all the way through Scripture God's Word and God's Spirit come together in order for God's Will to be done. They are as inseparable as fish and chips, love and marriage, Ant and Dec. Here are several examples:

- Right at the start of the Bible, the writer describes how God's Spirit was at work as the Creator spoke the creative word (Genesis 1).

- In the very next chapter, God speaks about making humans and breathes into Adam to animate him (the Hebrew word for breath can be translated 'Spirit')

- In Ezekiel 37, the prophet has a vision of dry bones in a valley. As he speaks the prophetic word, bodies come back together. Then he speaks and breath enters the dead bodies and they live. That word 'breath' again. Just in case we are in any doubt about what is happening, God explains that it's His Spirit that will cause the people to live (v14).

- When Jesus was baptised (Luke 3), The Spirit descends upon him and then God speaks words of affirmation over him.

- Jesus goes into the desert (Luke 4) 'full of the Holy Spirit' (v1) and during his time of testing by Satan he responds each time with the words of Scripture.

- The books of Ephesians and Colossians mirror each other in many ways. Ephesians 5:18 encourages us to be filled with the Spirit. Correspondingly in Colossians 3:16 the injunction is to allow the word of Christ to indwell us richly.

So there you have it. Now, on a practical level, how does engagement with the Word and the Spirit enable us to grow as disciples?

The Word

> *"Your word is a lamp for my feet, a light on my path"*
> *(Psalm 110:105).*

The primary channel through which God speaks to us is through Scripture: it is God's word to humanity. It's really important for us to grasp The Big Story of the Bible as well as the particular parts otherwise we can be in danger of reading into it what is not there! Having said that, there are those rare moments in our lives when God speaks through the words on the page in an 'out of context' way. I remember two times of crisis in my life when this has happened in a life altering manner. Let me tell the stories and then issue the cautions!

When our first son was born he was discovered to have a serious congenital heart problem. He was born by emergency caesarean section which meant that Sally was confined in hospital while Ben was in a special care unit for babies. Later in the day, having returned home for a couple of hours, I turned to the Lord in prayer about this awful situation. Opening my Bible to find my daily passage of scripture, this is what I read:

> *I will not die but live, and will proclaim what the LORD has done. (Psalm 118:17).*

When I returned to the hospital, Sally told me what her reading had been for that day:

> *For you created my inmost being;*
> *you knit me together in my mother's womb.*
> *I praise you because I am fearfully and wonderfully made;*
> *your works are wonderful,*
> *I know that full well.*
> *My frame was not hidden from you*
> *when I was made in the secret place,*
> *when I was woven together in the depths of the earth.*
> *Your eyes saw my unformed body;*
> *all the days ordained for me were written in your book*
> *before one of them came to be. (Psalm 139:13 – 16).*

These personal words from God sustained us through some traumatic episodes during Ben's early months, especially when it looked like we might lose him. Today he is a married man with three very handsome and intelligent sons (not that we are biased in any way...).

The second experience was just as remarkable but in an even stranger way.

I was working in ministry for Youth for Christ in the city of Derby. The National Director invited me to join the national team and take on a travelling brief. The only challenge was that there was no salary and therefore I would have to 'live by faith': in other words, I would have to trust God for all of our financial needs as a family.

The next morning I sat down to talk with the Lord, my Bible on my knee. I explained to Him that if I was going to do this, I needed to know that this is something He was leading me into. Now, I was young and immature, but I had recently discovered that John Wesley had once used 'Bible Bingo' as a way of getting divine guidance, so why not? I prayed and then flicked my Bible open somewhere in the New Testament. Looking at the page, the first phrase I saw read "The righteous shall live by faith". Scared silly, I slammed the Bible shut, my heart beating as if I had just finished running the Olympic 400 metres. I thought I'd better try again, but this time I would open it in the Old Testament section. Semi randomly, I opened towards the front end and looked down at the page and read "The righteous shall live by faith". I discovered later that this phrase occurs only three or four times in the whole Bible depending on which translation you are reading and I had 'accidently' found it twice in two openings.

From that moment, I knew that God would provide for all our practical needs. And He did. Sally and I spent twelve years living this way only ever asking the Lord for what we needed, no one else. My memory is a bit hazy but I can only remember being overdrawn at the Bank on one occasion by about 47p and even then it was my fault for forgetting to pay in a cheque. As you can imagine, it was quite an adventure!

Now, having told these two stories I want to emphasise that this type of biblical guidance is the exception, not the rule. And even when these things occurred, we were quick to check out with our good friends and church leaders that we were not simply hearing what we wanted to hear. Generally I have discovered that God disciples us through his Word when we engage in six particular ways:[19]

---

[19] I believe it was through an organisation called the Navigators that I first learnt this approach.

• **Read it.** Taking in some scripture on a regular basis is as important spiritually and morally as is taking food on board. The joyful discipline of spending some time alone with God and his Word on a daily basis will build you up. Usually during these times you will only read a paragraph or two, so try and find some other space and read through a whole book. You might read through the whole Bible in a year but if that is a step too far, try reading through the whole New Testament.

• **Hear it.** There are all kinds of Bible apps out there which enable you to listen to it being read. I sometimes use this when I'm on a long car journey and even when I'm doing some ironing! It's as if you can take a bath in the scriptures by letting the words wash over you. You may not be getting intensely into the finer points of the text, but something is going deep into your soul which will have its result in future times.

• **Memorise it.** In Psalm 119:11 we read:

I have hidden your word in my heart that I might not sin against you.

There is something about memorising parts of the Bible which gives you strength to follow Jesus, or ammunition to fight against evil. Remember again how Jesus's response to the devil when he was in the wilderness was always "It is written..." Even the Son of God had hidden the word of God in his heart and mind.

• **Meditate on it.** When a cow eats grass it does not go straight through the cow's system: the cow brings it back up and 'chews the cud' in order to extract maximum benefit. Meditating on scripture is spiritually chewing the cud. Here's an example:

Take the first few words of Psalm 23 "The Lord is my shepherd...". Now turn the phrase over in your mind with different emphases:

"THE LORD is my shepherd..." Think about who the Lord is.

"The Lord is MY shepherd..." You have the privilege of friendship.

"The Lord is my SHEPHERD..." A good shepherd does what for his sheep?

So, you are turning it over, mulling it over with thankfulness and questioning, squeezing all that you can out of this portion of God's word.

• **Study it.** There are so many levels at which you can delve deeper. It could be as simple as doing a personal study on a particular person or theme in the Bible, looking up all the references and making notes about what you learn and how it applies. These days there are all sorts of Bible study tools online, just beware that you are not looking at some crazy, heretical extremist material; an older believer can probably guide you. And, of course, you can dive into the Word at a whole different level through taking a degree or doing Masters level study; there's a thought!

• **Act on it!** Five frogs were sitting on a log in a pond. Four decided to dive in. How many were left on the log? The answer is...five. Deciding to do something is not the same thing as doing it! God is looking for biblical activists, those who 'do the Word'. You will remember the parable Jesus told about the wise man and the foolish man who built houses, one on rock and one on sand (Matthew 7:24 – 27). In the story both men heard the word of the Lord. The reason why the house built on rock survived the rain, storms and wind was, said Jesus because the wise man "... hears these words of mine and puts them into practice."

In the same way, James encourages believers "Do not merely listen to the word, and so deceive yourselves. Do what it says." (James 1:22).

If all we do is read, hear, meditate, memorise and study the Bible but not obey what God says, then we will simply become spiritually and morally obese!

One last thing to mention in all of this: what is the main point of engaging with the Bible? Certainly it's to equip you and to strengthen you as you discover God's ways, promises and directions for flourishing. Above and beyond even these wonderful benefits, the Bible is there to reveal more of Jesus to us. He said:

> *"You study the Scriptures diligently because you think that in them you have eternal life. These are the very Scriptures that testify about me, yet you refuse to come to me to have life." (John 5:39, 40).*

On the road to Emmaus:

> *...beginning with Moses and all the Prophets, he explained to them what was said in all the Scriptures concerning himself. (Luke 24:27)*

So as you read, listen, memorise, meditate and study the Bible, pray that more than anything you will have an increasing understanding in your heart and mind of who Jesus really is. The more you see of him, the more you will love him, honour him and follow him as a true disciple. And as you choose obedience to the Word of the Lord, the Lord of the Word will be revealed in a greater and deeper way. Obedience and revelation of Jesus are a continuing upward spiral.

The Spirit

Nearly every human, unless they have some strange sociopathic tendencies, has a sense of what is morally right and wrong. We know how we should live; the challenge is doing it. God is in the business of transformation, of changing us from the inside out. His laws which at one time were etched on tablets of stone are being embedded into our hearts through the Holy Spirit. As we have already discussed, He is the one who makes available to us His gifts and causes us to live fruitfully and flourishingly in this world.

In John 16, Jesus describes how when he goes back to the Father he will send the *Parakletos* to them (v7). This Greek word is translated in several ways: Advocate, Counsellor, Comforter, Helper. It literally means 'one who stands alongside'. At the time of writing, we (well, Sally really) are trying to grow a couple of tomato plants and a sunflower in the back yard. They have all had stakes or canes attached to them in order to offer support, strength and encouragement to the plants. Hopefully this will help the plants to grow to maturity and produce something. Well, the Holy Spirit is like a strong stake, holding us up even when we feel weak and impotent. The great news is that not only is He with us, He is in us so that we can receive power and strength to live for Christ as witnesses, disciples (Acts 1:8, Ephesians 3:16).

In this sense, the Spirit is the perfect discipler who not only reveals Jesus to us but then enables us to emulate the Lord albeit to a limited degree.

In closing out this chapter, I want to emphasise how critical it is to experience the Spirit and Word of God at work in our lives symbiotically, in tandem if you like. If we only rely on the Bible for our training and equipping we will be in danger of the sin of Bibliolatry where we elevate scripture to a place of worship. The end result will be that we live out a dry, lifeless, legalistic, religious existence. Conversely, if we choose to rely only on what God tells us in a spooky, over-spiritualised fashion, we will create religious anarchy in the Church. The apostle Paul shows clearly how both agents of God hold together when he tells Timothy:

> *All Scripture is God-breathed and is useful for teaching,*
> *rebuking, correcting and training in righteousness...*
> *(2 Timothy 3:16).*

Again, Spirit and breath are related terms. In a similar way that God breathed into Adam to create life, He breathes His Spirit through the written Word and brings it to life and reveals particular relevance in our lives.

As we draw near to God, He speaks to us and, because He is close, we feel His breath. In fact without breath, He cannot speak.

The great evangelist David Watson put it this way:

> *"All Word and no Spirit, we dry up; all Spirit and no*
> *Word, we blow up; both Word and Spirit, we grow up."*

Discipleship is all about growing up!

For Reflection/Discussion

1. Think of a time when God has spoken to you through Scripture. How did you know it was God speaking?

2. Which of the six approaches to Bible engagement do you need to incorporate into your routine? How will you ensure this happens?

3. Is there a particular area of your life at the moment where you need the Holy Spirit's help to strengthen and equip you?

4. What ongoing steps will you take to allow God's Word and Spirit to adjust and transform you?

DISCIPLESHIP PROCESSES AND APPROACHES
Essential Issues for Discipler and Disciple

There is a difference between coaching, mentoring and discipleship, although there are all sorts of similarities and crossover points.

Coaching largely entails <u>drawing out</u> of a person what it is the person wants to or needs to achieve in a particular area of life. The coach's role is primarily to assist in this venture through careful listening and analysis of what is being expressed. Powerful questioning can open up areas of potential which need to be realised.

Mentoring is more concerned with the <u>pouring in</u> of wisdom, knowledge and training in order to maximise the effectiveness of the mentee in the sphere for which the mentoring is taking place. Whereas a coach does not necessarily need qualifications or expertise in the particular discipline being focused upon, a mentor needs to be at least involved in the field and, even better, to be ahead of the one being trained in terms of experience and career portfolio.

Discipleship involves all of the above but recognises some key distinctives:

- Each one of us should first and foremost recognise that we are disciples of Jesus Christ. We have seen earlier that there are a number of instances in the Scripture where a person was a disciple to another human being, but in order for what we do to be authentic, any discipling relationship must be undertaken 'in the Name of Jesus' meaning that it exhibits Christ-like hallmarks.

- Even though a discipleship process may be focused on a particular area of felt need e.g. to develop in a skill/gift or to deal with bad habits, it is recognised that biblically we are whole people and therefore we are body, soul and spirit. In some approaches to coaching or mentoring it may be possible to simply deal with a narrow area of life without addressing any other area. If this is done in a discipling relationship it may leave the process insufficiently addressed. For example, a mentor may help a chef become Michelin star in the restaurant, but if the chef is not behaving well at home this is not particularly the concern of the mentor. In discipleship the whole of life is of importance.

- It is possible to be coached or mentored without a strong relational bond to the person receiving input. Discipleship is about relationship and, at its best, shared lives. Certainly if it is happening in the local church and over a reasonably long period of time this should be the case. Words such as transparency, openness and vulnerability will become the hallmarks.

- There is a particular end goal in discipleship which is to assist someone to find new life in Christ and then to grow from immaturity towards a destination of Christlikeness. A basic principle in this is that the development of someone's character takes precedence over their growth in gifting: God is far more concerned about who we become over and above what we do. There are too many examples of Christian people who have been awesome in terms of their abilities but have failed to exhibit grace, holiness and all-round godliness in the workplace, home or church. I am aware that I have alluded to this earlier, but it cannot be overemphasised.

Some years ago when I was still involved in leading a local church, we had someone join us who, on the face of it, was a vibrant believer with great enthusiasm and a desire to be involved in church life and ministry. One day I was in the sauna at my gym and got chatting to a man. As I often did I asked him where he worked (this was also a way into him asking me what I did which gave me an opportunity to share something about Jesus!). He mentioned the company and I immediately responded by asking him "Oh, do you know -----------------------------? He has just joined our church!" A scowl came over the man's face. "Yes, I know him. He's a pig!" He went on to describe how this Christian brother dealt with staff unfairly, spoke harshly and acted as if he was entitled to be treated as someone very special. Of course the wind was taken completely out of my sails. How could I talk to this man about a God who transforms lives, turning bad habits into good practices and weakness into strength? I made my excuses and headed for the showers. No doubt the church guy had been trained in business how to manage the bottom line. He had learnt how to maximise output from staff. Sadly, no one had taught him to lead in the way of Jesus.

Similarly in church life, you may have noticed that when Paul outlines what qualifies someone for leadership he focuses pretty much exclusively on character qualities (1 Timothy 3, 2 Timothy 2:22-24, Titus 1:6-9). Given that this is the case for leaders, it should be the aspiration of anyone on a discipleship journey since we are called to follow the example set by those who lead.

I remember the late Barney Coombs, founder of the Salt and Light network of churches talking to Christian leaders and describing how there can be time bombs ticking away in our lives. He meant areas of moral deficiency which had never been exposed to the light and dealt with. Barney said that, since we are involved in spiritual warfare, the enemy of our souls is content to wait and will detonate the bomb when it will cause maximum damage to the Kingdom of God. How many times have we experienced this to be the case? Some minister who is well known in the community or even on a national platform ends up in disgrace usually because of misuse or abuse of money, sex or power. Sometimes all three.

Whether it's in church, the workplace or at home, God is concerned that we grow in integrity and grace. Transparent discipleship dilutes the potential for spiritual or moral crashes to occur.

Given these distinctives and issues, let's look at six practical/biblical areas which are critical for fruitful and effective discipleship.

1. The Ephesians 4 Dynamic

> *So Christ himself gave the apostles, the prophets, the evangelists, the pastors and teachers, to equip his people for works of service, so that the body of Christ may be built up until we all reach unity in the faith and in the knowledge of the Son of God and become mature, attaining to the whole measure of the fullness of Christ.*
> *(Ephesians 4:11-13)*

The five ministry gifts given by the ascended Lord to the Church are for a specific purpose; namely to train and facilitate the Church into becoming all that God intended it should be. It may not be necessary to have lots of women and men with these clear, consistent, fruitful and often full-time vocational ministries, but what they bring to God's people is critical.

First of all, every believer can be equipped to go into the world and exhibit something of these manifestations. Each one of us can:

✓ go into the world (apostolic)

✓ speak God's word (prophetic)

✓ share the Gospel (evangelistic)

✓ care for others (pastor, shepherd)

✓ communicate biblical truth (teach)

The five-fold ministries exist to equip every willing believer in these areas of service. The global Church tends to be overly led and influenced by the pastor/teacher model. If we are going to see God's people brought to unity and maturity we have to ensure that all five gifts from the ascended Christ are made room for in the Christian community!

The kind of training and development envisaged here can take place to some degree through a taught class or a course. But let's not think that simply because someone has a 'certificate of completion' that the job is done. The challenge is to encourage or facilitate a context where the one who has been taught can put into practice what has been learnt or imparted. So, for example, a short term mission trip either at home or overseas can assist in releasing the apostolic; or the opportunity to be involved in an outreach to a local community where the evangelistic, prophetic or pastoral gift could be utilized. There can be lots of creative ways to activate what has been deposited. Added to this, church leadership should ensure that there are scheduled events where the five-fold gifts can be taught and used ongoingly rather than once in a blue moon!

Alongside the equipping of the whole church, there are those who are embryonic ministries requiring development. Like a young child, there may be clear signs in someone that their temperament, approach and activity suggests something about their ministry trajectory in the future. For example, it's at least possible that Timothy was apostolic and so the Apostle Paul nurtured what was there.

In terms of maturity, how do we recognise that a person has a growing ministry in one of these areas? The simplest answer would be that 'the evidence of a ministry is fruitfulness'. I remember one occasion when a young man asked if we could have a coffee. Well, I'm always up for a shot or two of caffeine! He said that he was an evangelist and therefore wanted to pick my brains on how to increase the size of his ministry platform. In other words, how could he get more opportunities to preach! So I asked him if he could tell me about the last couple of times when he had led someone to faith in Christ. He looked at me as if I was speaking in Swahili! Eventually he said that he couldn't remember ever bringing someone through to a friendship with God but he had been 'mightily used' in sowing the seed of the Gospel. So, was he an evangelist? Probably not. And the sad thing was that he could have been missing what the Lord had really got planned for him. Similarly we can have a church led by someone who carries the title 'pastor' and yet most of the people feel insecure and uncared for. It could be that the leader really functions in one of the other gifts and has become a square peg in a round hole.

Taking a Bible verse out of context, Proverbs 18:16 says '...a man's gift makes room for him...' Now this means if you take a present or some money along, you may well gain access to some people or place where otherwise you wouldn't find a hearing. But just to be slightly naughty for a moment, spiritually the same principle operates. If we truly carry an Ephesians 4:11 ministry, it will open doors of opportunity for us to serve the Lord.

Jesus told Kingdom parables concerning mustard seeds and yeast. There is a principle here about things beginning in a small way and growing over time. The same is true so often in an individual's life and ministry. It's been my privilege to preach the Gospel in some very large settings, but my first opportunity was in a small mission church on the social housing estate where I grew up. I still remember getting up to speak with my notes written out by hand on fourteen sheets of A4 paper. As I placed them on the lectern, someone opened a door and a gust of wind blew the papers across the platform. As they fell to the floor, the papers almost miraculously shuffled themselves in a totally random manner. Normal service was postponed for at least three minutes while I rearranged the transcript! Often in those late-teenage years I would have the chance to preach to a church congregation consisting of three or four people in an old draughty building on a cold February Sunday evening. But those experiences began to hone the gift of evangelism in me, to sharpen it. By the age of 22 when I joined Youth for Christ, I had been preaching for four years in churches, coffee bars and anywhere else I could find an audience.

You may have a strong sense of motivation and vision to be used by God in one particular area that's been outlined above. Start where you are, with godly ambition and see where the Lord takes you. Having outlined all of this, it's worth saying that the majority of mature believers tend to be a mixture of the five ministry areas with particular strength perhaps in a couple of them. Let me underline here that those with a narrow ministry are the exception not the rule.

Importantly, let's also recognise that these gifts are not meant to be locked up in our church services or to operate only in 'spiritual' contexts. These gifts need to be recognised and encouraged in the workplace, in our education system, in politics, etc. Others may not recognise them as such, but as God's people we should affirm that there are apostles, prophets, evangelists, pastors and teachers who the Lord has seeded out into the wider world. The London Institute of Contemporary Christianity have produced lots of resources to assist believers in living out the faith between Monday and Saturday.[20]

2. The Choice

It appears to be the case that in New Testament times, the common approach to becoming a disciple was to ask someone to take you on. In particular this was the case for young men who wished to become rabbis.

When it comes to asking someone for input and training in terms of character development or spiritual enhancement, there are a couple of obvious steps to take. First of all, pray and ask God to guide you. Second, write down some ideas of what it is you would want to gain from this kind of relationship.

Don't rush these first two steps. Give yourself some time to reflect, pray and clarify what it is you believe God requires of you at this stage in your walk with Jesus. You cannot, for example, jump overnight from rarely having a devotional time to three hours in the Bible and prayer every day.

At this point, ask to see someone from your church leadership team so that you can chat it through and get some counsel and maybe some suggestions about who would be a good discipler for you at this time. If you are passionate and straining to go forwards, you may have already decided that the best person to equip you is the senior leader of your church. Now, wait: this person is probably already busting a gut to keep up with existing priorities! So don't try and pressure the leader into something. If you do, you may well both end up being disappointed with the results.

---

[20] *www.licc.org.uk*

Unless you have a clear call into church ministry as a job, broadening this out into a whole life scenario, who would you ask to train you? Imagine that you wanted to become an electrician. Would you apprentice yourself to a hairdresser? I believe we have missed a trick here. Within the Christian Church we have strong believers functioning in all kinds of careers. What if you could link up with someone who has progressed in the workplace and remained loyal to Christ? That could end up being a much more helpful fit.

So it's perfectly legitimate for you to carefully and humbly look for someone to disciple you. In the New Testament, it seems that some people were given an option to choose to be disciples of Jesus as long as they had weighed up the implications (Luke 9:23), but the radical difference with Rabbi Jesus was that he tended to do the choosing (Matthew 4:19, 20). Similarly, it seems as if Paul chose Timothy to go with him and be equipped (Acts 16:1-3).

The leadership guru, John Maxwell makes the point that leadership is summed up in one word: ***influence.*** If you have a certain level of maturity (it doesn't have to be measured in years!) and you have the confidence of the senior leader(s) in your church, maybe you should be asking the Lord:

> *"Who can I influence? Who should I reach out to and seek to disciple?"*

On a practical level, it's worth checking out whether what you sense finds resonance with church leadership before you make an approach to someone. Make it relatively easy for the person to decline; it needs to be non-coercive. The prospective disciple needs to hear God about this as well as you!

3. Discipler/Disciple Characteristics

What should you be looking for in someone who will train and equip you? First of all, have they themselves been discipled? Do they know experientially what it's like? If not there is the potential for them to be either too demanding or too easy on you! Then, are they someone who has been given authority to do this by church leaders? The story in Matthew 8:5-13 concerning the Roman centurion is helpful. He recognised that if you are under authority, this gives you authority rather than it simply being something you have assumed for yourself. Next, do you feel you can voluntarily give them the right to speak into your life? This is not to say that you must always accept the counsel and advice offered, but if it turns out that a lot of the time you cannot or will not take on board what is being suggested, there is a swift end coming to this relationship! Added to this, do you have a sense that this person is for you? That he/she wants the best for you? That they are on your side? Finally, do they present a good example of godly character and action? Whether it's genetic or spiritual, we reproduce after our own kind, so what will be imparted to you from this friendship?

If you are the one tasked with helping someone grow, what should you be looking for? It depends of course on what point in the discipleship journey the person has reached, but I offer the following. They should be someone who is willing to learn from you. If you constantly hear them saying 'Yes, I already know that/do that.' when you are trying to adjust something, there is a challenge! They should not be so independent that you can't lead them in any sense, but neither are you looking for someone to become over dependent on you. What we want to produce is someone who chooses to be accountable for their actions and attitudes but still takes responsibility for who they are. They should be servant-hearted since this is what we are all aiming for. When God became human, he took the nature of a servant (Philippians 2:7), so should we. I'm reminded of the film 'Karate Kid' when Mr Miyagi agrees to train Daniel in the martial arts. Daniel's first two sessions involved painting a fence and polishing a car. Servanthood! What Daniel didn't realise was the value these disciplines would have later on – watch the film! Lastly, they should be faithful and trustworthy. Jesus taught about those who are trustworthy in small ways end up getting more (Luke 16:10). If the one you are seeking to equip says they are going to do something and consistently fails to do it, there is a massive integrity gap.

Having said this, none of us are the finished article, so let's be aware that in going for the ideal we don't miss out on the reality of people being human, broken and flawed!

4. The Deal

It's amazing how much we forget over time and how often what we 'remember' differs between two parties. For this reason, even though this relationship will be undergirded by friendship and mutual respect, I suggest a written record is prepared of what was agreed at the beginning. What should be included?

- A start and finish date – When? Until?
- Expected outcomes – What?
- The means by which these will be achieved – How?
- Regularity of meeting up and the means of access.
- Responsibilities of discipler/disciple – Expectations.
- Possible reasons for a termination.
- Who to contact if there is a problem – an 'honest broker'.
- Other issues particular to the circumstances.

5. Training, not Teaching

The aim is to produce disciples, not academic theologians!

Now I wouldn't want anyone to misunderstand me here. I have taught undergraduates at theological college for nearly sixteen years and I am an advocate of robust biblical education, personally holding a Master's degree in Applied Theology. My point is that it's possible to be educated about God but not to be a disciple. Experience with hundreds of students gives me all the evidence I need! Most of them seem to navigate through and grow in godliness as well as receiving a degree, but the two issues are not necessarily synonymous.

Equally I would suggest that the pulpit on Sunday is not the primary place to make disciples. When we preach and teach, we believe that God can take His Word and apply it to individual lives. We also believe that the Holy Spirit can use the sermon to illuminate, convict, encourage, save. Most of this takes place in crisis moments as people sit listening to us opening up God's Truth and this is vital ministry. But discipleship requires process, not a series of one-off encounters on a once a week basis. Discipleship facilitates the earthing, the nailing down of what is being taught Sunday by Sunday.

Training by its very nature entails doing something. It's difficult to train something if it doesn't move! Jesus and his disciples would be 'exhibit A' in this. They were moving around, learning how to preach, pray, heal, deliver, find a bed for the night, feed the masses, find a tied up ass, book an upper room. In the midst of all this, the edges were being knocked off them and shaping was taking place. They still needed teaching from the Lord and ultimately they needed the power of the Holy Spirit to put it all together, but what is clear is that this was not classroom stuff!

6. How Many?

What size of group works best for this kind of training? It depends; 1, 3, 12 or 72?

There is no clear record of Jesus having a long term exclusive discipling relationship with just one person, but you can imagine that over the three year period when they were moving around there was plenty of time for him to have some more in depth conversations with individuals about their lives. Now this is a case being made from the silence of Scripture and this makes it somewhat tentative. The only obvious occasion where a private, loving confrontation took place was when Jesus walked on the beach with Peter and asked him the same question three times (John 21:15-19). There are, however other examples which seem to be one-on-one such as Paul and Timothy or Elijah and Elisha.

There is a potential danger in this kind of usually very intense discipleship, mainly to do with exclusivity and the perception of a leader showing favouritism to someone to the detriment of others. I wonder whether 'behind the scenes' something like this was happening when Paul wrote to Timothy

> *Don't let anyone look down on you because you are young, but set an example for the believers in speech, in conduct, in love, in faith and in purity. (1 Timothy 4:12)*

Maybe some older believers were feeling left out by this 'father-son' relationship and were letting it be known!

It must also be pretty obvious that at this level, discipleship needs to be between those of the same sex in order to avoid potential misunderstandings or difficulties.

Even given the challenges and potential hiccups with this type of discipleship, there are times when this kind of 'hothouse' growth is appropriate particularly for strategic leadership reasons. This perhaps becomes clear when Paul later writes to Timothy and encourages him in this way:

> *...what you have heard from me in the presence of many witnesses entrust to faithful men who will be able to teach others also. (2 Timothy 2:2)*

Here we have a four generation discipleship push! There was something very longsighted in God's economy when he brought Paul and Timothy together.

In the Gospels it becomes clear that Peter, James and John were particularly close to Jesus and were privy to some things that the rest of the twelve missed out on. Similarly with Paul there were times when his apostolic team was quite small with others coming and going. The principle here is of a small group, less than a handful, who are drawn together for specific fellowship, training, equipping and for a particular task. In these kind of micro groupings, sometimes called 'huddles', it may well be that there is someone leading who is mainly responsible for discipling the others, but there is another possibility which we might term 'peer-to-peer' discipleship. Let me describe my own experience of this below.

It's been a joy and privilege to be part of an accountability group with three other men for more than a decade. Recently one of our number, a godly man named Dave Ayling went to be with the Lord. At the time of writing it still doesn't feel real. We still grieve. There is no doubt that Jason, Mark and I will carry on. We need each other. The only human person who knows me better than these guys is my wife! There is an honesty and accountability which I need. We physically meet up maybe six times a year for a whole day, but in between we talk often several times a week through video calls or texts. I know that if I had an issue I couldn't handle alone, they would be there as soon as possible. I commend this micro-community idea to you, particularly if you are in any kind of leadership capacity in church or in 'the real world'.

We are all aware of Jesus and the twelve. In our contemporary world this might be seen as the equivalent of a cell, life group, house group, whatever this small group dynamic is called in your church. This is arguably the key community for local church discipleship. At its best it can be a place for openness, challenge, vulnerability, support, mission, training, adjustment, etc.

Nearly every study conducted on the characteristics of a healthy church concludes that holistic small groups are massively important. The danger is that unless these groups and their leaders are encouraged, resourced and held accountable for what goes on, they often 'swerve to rot' to quote my good friend Laurence Singlehurst[21].

There is an unfortunate tendency for a small group to end up becoming made in the likeness of its leader. So, if this person is primarily a pastor it becomes a care group. If the leader is a teacher it tends towards Bible study. When the leader is evangelistic it becomes an outreach group. A prophetic type will create a group

---

[21] *www.celluk.org.uk*

where everyone gets prayed for almost every week and receives 'a word'.

For this reason, small groups need to be vision-driven and purpose-driven rather than small group leader-driven! At its simplest, the old UP-IN-OUT paradigm can work well meaning the group becomes a place for worship, word and witness and the three are balanced. But even then we need to realise that not every time we gather do we have to do the 'same old same old' otherwise things can become stale. It really is OK to go to the cinema together, or for a summer evening picnic in a park, etc. From a discipleship point of view there is opportunity to hold each other to account for how we are each attempting to do UP-IN-OUT in our personal lives. There is also opportunity to have seasons where we choose as a group to develop in an area of Christian practice such as fasting, meditation, solitude, etc.

As iron sharpens iron, so one person sharpens another.
(Proverbs 27:17)

As I write this, the world is in the grip of the Covid-19 pandemic and church leaders are in the midst of working out how we 'do church' in the inevitable 'new normal' which will follow. Yesterday I listened to a podcast featuring an old friend, Jeff Lucas, who over the past, say, thirty years has been massively influential in the Christian Church. Jeff mentioned a call he had recently with the leader of one of the five biggest churches in the USA with 37,000 members (one church in many locations). With all the challenges of church lockdown, this leader told Jeff that they had hardly missed a beat, primarily because they had built the church on a foundation of small groups. Going forward, this has to be a major key in how we make disciples, provide true fellowship, enable the release of spiritual gifts and manifest God's Kingdom more effectively.

Last of all, Jesus had the seventy two in Luke 10:1. They are not explicitly referred to as disciples but they seem to have been around Jesus and he appoints and sends them out in twos to preach and heal. When they return he tells them that their names are written in Heaven, so something good is going on for them!

In recent years there has been the growth of churches organising themselves around 'missional communities'. The idea here has been to engage with God's mission in groups which are small enough for everyone to feel a sense of belonging but big enough to make a 'Kingdom splash' into a neighbourhood or a particular network of people. Usually these missional communities will aim to be between thirty and seventy strong. The clear aim is to make disciples and to be disciples themselves so typically they will configure around 'huddles' (micro community), cells and communities.

One of the radical aspects of these churches is that they do not necessarily do meetings on a weekly cycle or even a monthly cycle since they do not want to fill everyone's time and energy up with Christian gatherings. One such church, Kings Church Warrington[22] tends to work on a half termly basis and, even though they may have a Sunday morning celebration service each week, not all the missional communities would be there, depending on what was happening with them as a community. It may be that by the time you read this they have changed the way they operate, such is the vision and desire to be led by the missional Spirit of God and to make disciples.

What becomes quite clear from the above is that the more specific, deep and sacrificial the equipping, the smaller the group context is in which it operates. Rick Warren observed that church needs to grow bigger and smaller at the same time. Now, there's something to ponder!

---

[22] *www.kingschurchwarrington.co.uk*

For Reflection/Discussion

1. Why is there a lack of intentional discipleship in the Church?

2. Why are character qualities more important than giftedness?

3. Which of the five ministry areas would you exhibit most easily? How can you be matured in this?

4. How might your ministry strength be outworked in day-to-day life?

5. Could peer-to-peer discipleship work in your context? How could you set it up?

DISCIPLESHIP, THE LOCAL CHURCH AND THE FUTURE

A Final Word

As we come in to land at the end of this book, I wanted to finish by issuing a challenge mainly aimed at church leaders.

Recently, Sally and I celebrated forty years of marriage; woohoo! It was also within two days of her birthday and since it was all very special, I bought her a brand new iPad. The one she had been using was basically steam-driven and had long since stopped doing software updates. In short, the existing operating system was not fit for purpose; it needed a different mode of operation.

Even though on a global level we are seeing massive, unprecedented growth in the Christian church, here in the West we are in serious decline. It's true that the Pentecostal/charismatic/evangelical churches are doing better, but in absolute terms it is still marginal growth.

So what's the answer? A major part of the answer it seems to me is that we need a new operating system which will internally change our hearts and vision and will externally cause us to restructure how we 'do church' as the people of God.

All of this must start where the Lord Jesus began and actually where he finished his earthly ministry, namely by making disciples. Of course we can debate exactly what this means and how we do it, but the bottom line must be whether we are being church in such a way that people are enabled, trained and empowered to become more and more like Jesus.

Mike Breen has been quoted extensively in recent years:

> *"If you make disciples, you always get the church. But if you make a church, you rarely get disciples."*[23]

---

[23] M. Breen. *Building a Discipleship Culture* (3dm International, 2017).

Let's be careful that we are not deceived into thinking that the most important issue we have is to fill all the seats in our church buildings on Sunday. We can go for 'bums, buildings, bucks and buzz' as the measures of how well we are doing. Important as these markers may be, they must not be, cannot be the main focus of what we are about.

Here is how the process should operate: if we make disciples, out of that pool we will end up discovering more ministries and more leaders. If we discover more ministries and leaders we will have healthier disciple-making churches. The disciples from these churches will go and plant the Gospel into unreached communities both at home and across the nations. And then the end will come (Matthew 24:14).

If our focus is mainly on what happens on a Sunday morning for an hour or two, we will at best form truncated disciples. Now I love the gathering of God's family for powerful worship and teaching/preaching, and I believe in those moments of encounter and life change which can and do occur. But unless we have operating systems which offer accountability, shaping, challenge, mutual encouragement, transparency, authentic community and a compulsive call to reach lost people with God's Good News, well...

In the midst of the recent Covid-19 Pandemic, the Church has found itself having to operate in a radically different mode due to government restrictions on meeting together in a traditional way on Sundays or midweek. At the time of writing (Summer 2021), it's impossible to know with any degree of certainty how this will affect the corporate configurations of church meetings in the years ahead. In the USA where churches have begun services, the numbers attending have been slashed, particularly in the larger congrgations. Now this could be explained simply because people are being cautious about attendance since the virus is still quite rampant over there. Interestingly the churches in Guernsey in the Channel Islands found that they were rammed full as they have returned from lockdown after the virus had been pretty much eliminated on the island.

Will we find that the 'new normal' in the West will not be that different to how it was before the Pandemic once the level of infection becomes extremely low or when the vaccines are completely rolled out? Will we discover that those unchurched people who have tuned in to an online service will arrive at our buildings once we fully re-open? Maybe some believers will decide that they prefer something more organic and grassroots in terms of church style and a mushrooming of small-scale church planting will take place? Will online church become a really big thing? No one knows at present; it's so difficult to predict. Whatever happens, the challenge of effective disciple making will remain and we will need lots of creative thinking, action and resourcing to make it happen.

Thank God that even before the COVID crisis we were seeing signs of a fresh commitment in our churches to change the operating system! Going forwards there will be a need for very flexible approaches in our desire to make fully-formed Jesus followers utilising online tools, webinars, podcasts and the whole variety of social media now available to us. Even if social distancing remains a thing for some time or if other viral crises arise in the future, the creative Spirit of God will surely help us to navigate through and create meaningful and fruitful discipleship pathways. I am full of faith that in the years ahead we will grasp the nettle more than ever and change whatever needs changing for the sake of the King and his Kingdom. Amen?

APPENDIX. 'THE WALK'.

A Nurture Course for New Believers

Rick Warren from Saddleback Church in USA has a way with words. I once heard him say this:

> *"A great commitment to the Great Command and the Great Commission will produce a Great Church."*

Not only is that a brilliant saying, it is true! It's just as true when we personalise it to making great disciples.

When I originally wrote The Walk, I wanted every section to implicitly be part of a drop-down menu from the Great Command (love God, love your neighbour. Mark 12:30, 31) and the Great Commission (Go and make disciples. Matthew 28:18-20). For example:

- Why share your faith with someone? Because you love your neighbour and you have been commissioned.

- Why read the Bible? Because you love God and want to find out more about Him.

- Why church? Because you love the Father and His family.

- Why be baptised? Because you love God and therefore want to be obedient.

- Why be filled with the Holy Spirit? Because if you are going to love your neighbour, you need God's power.

What became clear early on in the prototypes for this course was that the new believer needed to deal with some basic foundations even before getting into the areas mentioned above. For instance, some people have a powerful experience with God and form an authentic connection with Him, but there is a need to be deprogrammed from years of thinking that God is not good or that He wants to remain aloof and distant from us. Then there is the issue of Lordship; who is in charge of my life now? The new disciple also has to discover quickly that the Trinity is there to give them lots of help as they journey forwards.

You will discover that I have attempted not to give the answers away. The scriptures are largely contained within the booklet and I am trusting that the Holy Spirit will guide the person to the truth as the new Jesus follower engages with God's Word. By the way, one of the main reasons for including the scripture passages is firstly in case the person does not possess a Bible and, if they do, I wanted to ensure it was an understandable version! Secondly, if the course is being run in a small group setting, new believers can be very embarrassed if the leader says 'turn to Ephesians chapter two' and the newbie has no idea where to look!

I have been asked why I included a section on money. In the West, money and material things are often what we obsess over. They are our idols which need smashing early on if we are to walk strongly with Jesus. So it was very deliberate. Martin Luther said that there are three necessary conversions: the heart, the mind and the purse. This is probably more the case now than ever!

So, what follows is the complete Course, minus its jacket cover!

Copies of the full booklet **'The Walk. Becoming a Jesus Follower'** are available direct from gary.gibbs@elim.org.uk. At the time of writing they cost £3 each plus postage and packing.

THE WALK

BECOMING A JESUS FOLLOWER

BY GARY GIBBS

THE WALK
BECOMING A JESUS FOLLOWER

Design & Photography by: samjacksonphoto.co
sam@samjacksonphoto.co

CONTENTS

WELCOME!

You are most likely to be reading this because recently you decided to become a follower of Jesus and you need to discover, experience and practice some of the foundational things involved in going forward on this Great Adventure!

There are twelve subjects covered in the course, each dealing with a foundation for becoming a more fully rounded Christian.
You can do the course alone, with a more mature believer or in a small group setting; whichever works best for you.
Here's a suggested way to engage with the study:

• Begin to read a section until you come to a space for you to write.
• Where there is a Bible passage, read it through twice, first at your usual reading speed and then more slowly.
• Answer any questions.
• Think about any issues raised.
• Be as honest as you can with yourself!
• If you have someone helping you with the course, share with them what has helped you, confused you, challenged you or changed you!

All you need to get started is a pen or pencil and a modern version of the Bible.

Enjoy, and may God bless you!

P.S. Finding the part of the Bible to read can sometimes be tricky, so use the Contents page at the front of the Bible!

Also remember that if there's a number at the beginning of the part you're looking for, it means you need to be careful to find the right book. For example, John 3:16 is in John's Gospel after Matthew, Mark and Luke. 1John 3:16 is in John's first letter and is followed by 2John and 3John, his second and third letters. You will pick it up very quickly!

> **"We follow Jesus a step at a time, a day at a time..."**
> Warren Wiersbe

> **"Follow me"**
> Jesus of Nazareth

GOOD GOD!

What is God like? What sort of character is he?

• A cosmic policeman waiting for us to step out of line?
• A white-bearded old man who's a bit past it?
• A vindictive sadist dishing out pain on unsuspecting humans?

Answer? None of the above!

Fortunately, God has described himself for us. Almost every page of the Bible reveals more about who he is. But for now, here are the headlines:

1. He's Powerful and Creative

The very first chapter in the Bible shows us this:

'In the beginning God created the heavens and the earth. Now the earth was formless and empty, darkness was over the surface of the deep, and the Spirit of God was hovering over the waters.
God said, "Let there be light," and there was light. God saw that the light was good, and he separated the light from the darkness. God called the light "day," and the darkness he called "night." And there was evening, and there was morning - the first day.
And God said, "Let there be a vault between the waters to separate water from water." So God made the vault and separated the water under the vault from the water above it. And it was so. God called the vault "sky." And there was evening, and there was morning - the second day. And God said, "Let the water under the sky be gathered to one place, and let dry ground appear." And it was so. God called the dry ground "land," and the gathered waters he called "seas." And God saw that it was good.
Then God said, "Let the land produce vegetation: seed-bearing plants and trees on the land that bear fruit with seed in it, according to their various kinds." And it was so. The land produced vegetation: plants bearing seed according to their kinds and trees bearing fruit with seed in it according to their kinds. And God saw that it was good. And there was evening, and there was morning -
the third day. And God said, "Let there be lights in the vault of the sky to sepa-rate the day from the night, and let them serve as signs to mark seasons and days and years, and let them be lights in the vault of the sky to give light on the

GOOD GOD!

earth." And it was so. God made two great lights - the greater light to govern the day and the lesser light to govern the night. He also made the stars. God set them in the vault of the sky to give light on the earth, to govern the day and the night, and to separate light from darkness. And God saw that it was good. And there was evening, and there was morning - the fourth day. And God said, "Let the water teem with living creatures, and let birds fly above the earth across the vault of the sky." So God created the great creatures of the sea and every living and moving thing with which the water teems, according to their kinds, and every winged bird according to its kind. And God saw that it was good. God blessed them and said, "Be fruitful and increase in number and fill the water in the seas, and let the birds increase on the earth." And there was evening, and there was morning - the fifth day. And God said, "Let the land produce living creatures according to their kinds: livestock, creatures that move along the ground, and wild animals, each according to its kind." And it was so. God made the wild animals according to their kinds, the livestock according to their kinds, and all the creatures that move along the ground according to their kinds. And God saw that it was good. Then God said, "Let us make human beings in our image, in our likeness, so that they may rule over the fish in the sea and the birds in the sky, over the livestock and all the wild animals, and over all the creatures that move along the ground." So God created human beings in his own image, in the image of God he created them; male and female he created them.'

Genesis 1:1-28

Which words here show that God is powerful and creative?

GOOD GOD!

2. He's Good and Loving

"The LORD is compassionate and gracious, slow to anger, abounding in love.
He will not always accuse, nor will he harbour his anger forever;
he does not treat us as our sins deserve or repay us according
to our iniquities.
For as high as the heavens are above the earth, so great is his love for those
who fear him; as far as the east is from the west, so far has he removed our
transgressions from us. As a father has compassion on his children, so the
LORD has compassion on those who fear him; from everlasting to everlasting
the LORD's love is with those who fear him, and his righteousness with their
children's children— with those who keep his covenant and remember to obey
his precepts."

Psalm 103: 8 - 13 & 17

In a sentence, what does this Psalm tell you about God?

How is this different to the way many people think about God?

3. He's Holy

"As obedient children, do not conform to the evil desires you had when you
lived in ignorance. But just as he who called you is holy, so be holy in all you
do; for it is written: 'Be holy, because I am holy.'"

1 Peter 1: 14 – 16

131

GOOD GOD!

The word 'holy' means to be separate, distinct, pure. In what ways is God holy?

✎

Practically, how would being holy change the way you live?

✎

A Prayer

Lord, I think my understanding of who you are has been limited! Please help me to grasp hold of you as the Great Creator of everything. So many people think either that you don't exist or that you're not very nice. I want to know you for who you really are and not just my old ideas. Thank you that you accept me as I am, but you care so much for me that you will help me change and become more the person you made me to be.

Amen

FRIENDS

Why did God create human beings? It's a massive question and difficult to give a full answer here. For starters, here are a few things worth remembering:

1. He didn't make us because he was lonely!

The eternal God has always existed as a community. Christians believe this hard-to-understand thing:
There is one God who exists in three persons - Father, Son and Holy Spirit - sometimes called 'The Trinity'.

'Then God said, "Let us make human beings in our image, in our likeness, so that they may rule over the fish in the sea and the birds in the sky, over the livestock and all the wild animals, and over all the creatures that move along the ground." So God created human beings in his own image, in the image of God he created them; male and female he created them.'

Genesis 1: 26-27

"May the grace of the Lord Jesus Christ, and the love of God, and the fellowship of the Holy Spirit be with you all."

2 Corinthians 13:14

What do the above Bible verses show you about God?

FRIENDS

2. He made us to enjoy friendship with him

The Garden of Eden story in Genesis 3 speaks of God "walking in the garden in the cool of the day" (verse 8). In other words, he wanted to be with Adam and Eve. It was their disloyalty to him that spoilt the relationship.

But all through the Bible, God reminds us of how he wants it to be.

Look up these Bible verses and write down what each one indicates about God wanting friendship with us.

Lamentations 3:22, 23

Matthew 6:6 – 13

John 3:16

FRIENDS

3. He wants us to know he really loves us!

The world translated 'love' in the New Testament means more than simply a feeling. Rather, it is to do with commitment, loyalty and sacrifice. It means that God doesn't change in the amount or quality of his care for us.
It is consistent and complete.

The Father, Son and Holy Spirit each help us to know that we are loved in this way.

Look up each Bible verse and comment on what it says to you.

1 John 3:1

1 John 3:16

FRIENDS

Romans 5:5

✏️

Father, it's amazing to think that you, the Creator of the Universe, love me and wants this close friendship with me. Help me Lord to be a faithful friend to you.

Lord Jesus, thank you for giving up your life for me. I'm humbled by your love.

Holy Spirit, please keep pouring more and more of God's love into my heart. Thank you for making it all real.

Amen

RULES, RULES, RULES...

We hated them when we were at school. We occasionally break them a little when we're driving (!!). Most of us have 'bent' them at some time or other. But rules are usually good and helpful, not bad and disruptive! For example, imagine I continued typing this now but ditched the rules on grammar and punctuation... the result would be very messy!

1. God's Rules

'And God spoke all these words:
"I am the LORD your God, who brought you out of Egypt, out of the land of slavery.
"You shall have no other gods before me.
"You shall not make for yourself an image in the form of anything in heaven above or on the earth beneath or in the waters below. You shall not bow down to them or worship them; for I, the LORD your God, am a jealous God, punishing the children for the sin of the parents to the third and fourth generation of those who hate me, but showing love to a thousand generations of those who love me and keep my commandments.
"You shall not misuse the name of the LORD your God, for the LORD will not hold anyone guiltless who misuses his name.
"Remember the Sabbath day by keeping it holy. Six days you shall labour and do all your work, but the seventh day is a Sabbath to the LORD your God. On it you shall not do any work, neither you, nor your son or daughter, nor your male or female servant, nor your animals, nor any foreigner residing in your towns. For in six days the LORD made the heavens and the earth, the sea, and all that is in them, but he rested on the seventh day. Therefore the LORD blessed the Sabbath day and made it holy.
"Honour your father and your mother, so that you may live long in the land the LORD your God is giving you.
"You shall not murder.
"You shall not commit adultery.
"You shall not steal.
"You shall not give false testimony against your neighbour.
You shall not covet your neighbour's house. You shall not covet your neighbour's wife, or his male or female servant, his ox or donkey, or anything that belongs to your neighbour."'

Exodus 20:1 – 17

RULES, RULES, RULES...

These were the 'Ten Commandments' given by God to the Israelites after he had set them free from Egypt.

How do you think our world would be a better place if we lived by these rules?

What stops us living up to these commandments?

Are there any in particular that you have broken?

How does that make you feel?

RULES, RULES, RULES...

2. Making it Simple

By the time of Jesus, these basic ten rules had been expanded to over six hundred!! The religious leaders of the day had taken God's good law and made it into a straightjacket.
Six hundred rules is way over the top. The Ten Commandments alone make us realise we have failed.

But then, Jesus makes God's rules very simple...

'One of the teachers of the law came and heard them debating. Noticing that Jesus had given them a good answer, he asked him, "Of all the commandments, which is the most important?" "The most important one," answered Jesus, "is this: 'Hear, O Israel: The Lord our God, the Lord is one. Love the Lord your God with all your heart and with all your soul and with all your mind and with all your strength.' The second is this: 'Love your neighbour as yourself.' There is no commandment greater than these." "Well said, teacher," the man replied. "You are right in saying that God is one and there is no other but him. To love him with all your heart, with all your understanding and with all your strength, and to love your neighbour as yourself is more important than all burnt offerings and sacrifices." When Jesus saw that he had answered wisely, he said to him, "You are not far from the kingdom of God." And from then on no one dared ask him any more questions.'

Mark 12:28 – 34

Is it easier to keep these two rules (or are they one rule?) than to keep the ten?

✏️

Can you imagine say, one obvious practical change in your lifestyle if you loved God more?

✏️

RULES, RULES, RULES...

If you loved (= cared for) your neighbour (= other people)
as much as yourself, what areas of your life would
be affected?

3. "This is Impossible!"

Correct! The standard is beyond any of us. Maybe that's the whole point.
Otherwise, just like those religious leaders, we might think we can keep the
rules and make ourselves acceptable to God.

4. So, Back to Basics!

God doesn't accept us because we keep the rules. He accepts us because
we have turned back to him and received his gift of forgiveness and a new
life.

Now, as Jesus followers, we are not so much 'Failures' as 'Learners'. God
wants to teach us and help us to love him and to love people.
He changes rules into promises. It's not that we have to love God and
others. Rather, we will love God and others!

As we follow Jesus, we will become more like him. It's a journey, sometimes
difficult, but definitely adventurous!

A Prayer

Lord, help me in the weeks ahead to learn how to keep this one Great
Command, to love you and to love people. Thank you that you forgive me
when I fail. I commit myself again to following you. Teach me your ways
and your values.

In Jesus Name, Amen

ALL THE HELP YOU NEED

"May the grace of the Lord Jesus Christ, and the love of God, and the fellowship of the Holy Spirit be with you all."

2 Corinthians 13:14

A car doesn't keep going for very long if it's tank is empty. Human beings won't live very long unless they can take onboard food and drink. Even a camel gives up eventually if there's no oasis in sight!

Spiritually, the same thing is true. We would not be able to follow Jesus if there was no resource to draw on. Thankfully, there is!

As we seek to live out the Great Command (love God/love others), here's God's help for us...

1. The Grace of Jesus

'Grace' means that even though we deserve nothing from God, he has given us his very best.

"For it is by grace you have been saved, through faith - and this is not from yourselves, it is the gift of God - not by works, so that no one can boast. For we are God's handiwork, created in Christ Jesus to do good works, which God prepared in advance for us to do."

Ephesians 2: 8 – 10

On what basis did God save, or rescue us?

What did you add in to God saving you?

141

ALL THE HELP YOU NEED

> **What has God prepared for us to do?**
>
> ✐

> **How will understanding this help you in fulfilling the Great Command?**
>
> ✐

2. The Love of God

"Dear friends, let us love one another, for love comes from God. Everyone who loves has been born of God and knows God. Whoever does not love does not know God, because God is love. This is how God showed his love among us: He sent his one and only Son into the world that we might live through him. This is love: not that we loved God, but that he loved us and sent his Son as an atoning sacrifice for our sins. Dear friends, since God so loved us, we also ought to love one another. No one has ever seen God; but if we love one another, God lives in us and his love is made complete in us."

1 John 4:7 – 12

> **What's the evidence that we know God?**
>
> ✐

ALL THE HELP YOU NEED

What should happen to us if we know God's love?

How did God show his love?

How will understanding this help you in fulfilling the Great Command?

ALL THE HELP YOU NEED

3. The Presence ('Fellowship') of the Holy Spirit

"For the Spirit God gave us does not make us timid, but gives us power, love and self-discipline."

2 Timothy 1:7

How will understanding this help you in fulfilling the Great Command?

A Prayer

Dear Lord, thanks so much for your grace, love and presence with me. You've given me so much. Help me to give my worship and adoration to you. And may your Spirit in me enable me to live the life you want me to live.

In Jesus Name, Amen

WHO IS IN CHARGE?

When we become Christians, we receive Jesus as our Lord and Saviour, or to put it another way, as our Leader and Forgiver.

"As the Father has loved me, so have I loved you. Now remain in my love. If you keep my commands, you will remain in my love, just as I have kept my Father's commands and remain in his love. I have told you this so that my joy may be in you and that your joy may be complete."

John 15:9 – 11

How do we stay aware of Jesus' love?

Ask the Lord to show you if there is an area of your life where you're not living obediently.

What should we be experiencing if we are loyal to Jesus?

We need to allow Jesus to be the Lord (Leader, Ruler) over every part of our lives.

WHO IS IN CHARGE?

1. Lord of our bodies

"Flee from sexual immorality. All other sins people commit are outside their bodies, but those who sin sexually sin against their own bodies. Do you not know that your bodies are temples of the Holy Spirit, who is in you, whom you have received from God? You are not your own; you were bought at a price. Therefore honour God with your bodies."

1Corinthians 6:18 - 20

What in particular is wrong use of our bodies in this passage?

How else might we deny the Lordship of Jesus over our bodies?

2. Lord of our mouths

"Make a tree good and its fruit will be good, or make a tree bad and its fruit will be bad, for a tree is recognized by its fruit. You brood of vipers, how can you who are evil say anything good? For out of the overflow of the heart the mouth speaks. Good people bring good things out of the good stored up in them, and evil people bring evil things out of the evil stored up in them. But I tell you that people will have to give account on the Day of Judgment for every empty word they have spoken. For by your words you will be acquitted, and by your words you will be condemned."

Matthew 12:33 – 37

WHO IS IN CHARGE?

> **Why is it so important what we allow to influence us?**

> **How can we get more 'good stuff' into our lives?**

3. Lord of our thinking

"Do not conform to the pattern of this world, but be transformed by the renewing of your mind. Then you will be able to test and approve what God's will is - his good, pleasing and perfect will."

Romans 12: 2-3

> **How does the 'renewing of our mind' affect how we live?**

WHO IS IN CHARGE?

What will be the result of being transformed in this way?

☑

---

4. Lord of everything

"In your relationships with one another, have the same attitude of mind Christ Jesus had: Who, being in very nature God, did not consider equality with God something to be used to his own advantage; rather, he made himself nothing by taking the very nature of a servant, being made in human likeness. And being found in appearance as a human being, he humbled himself by becoming obedient to death - even death on a cross! Therefore God exalted him to the highest place and gave him the name that is above every name, that at the name of Jesus every knee should bow, in heaven and on earth and under the earth, and every tongue acknowledge that Jesus Christ is Lord, to the glory of God the Father."

Philippians 2: 5 – 11

A Prayer

Lord Jesus Christ, one day everyone will know that you are the King of the whole Universe. Today, Lord, I choose to surrender to you my King. There are particular areas of my life where I need your Rule to break in. So let your Kingdom come in me more and more. May my obedience show my love for you.

In your Name, Amen

DRENCHED! (1)

At first glance, baptism for a new believer seems like a strange ritual – go into a tank of water dry and come out wet! So, what's it all about?

"When the people heard this, they were cut to the heart and said to Peter and the other apostles, "Brothers, what shall we do?" Peter replied, "Repent and be baptized, every one of you, in the name of Jesus Christ for the forgiveness of your sins. And you will receive the gift of the Holy Spirit. The promise is for you and your children and for all who are far off - for all whom the Lord our God will call." With many other words he warned them; and he pleaded with them, "Save yourselves from this corrupt generation." Those who accepted his message were baptized, and about three thousand were added to their number that day."

Acts 2: 37 – 41

Peter tells the crowd to do two things and then to receive someone

---

What two things did they need to do?

1.

2.

What did they need to receive?

DRENCHED! (1)

1. The Meaning of Baptism

"And now what are you waiting for? Get up, be baptized and wash your sins away, calling on his name"

Acts 22:16

"And this water symbolizes baptism that now saves you also—not the removal of dirt from the body but the pledge of a clear conscience toward God. It saves you by the resurrection of Jesus Christ, who has gone into heaven and is at God's right hand—with angels, authorities and powers in submission to him."

1 Peter 3: 21-22

What sort of 'wash' does Baptism give you?

"What shall we say, then? Shall we go on sinning so that grace may increase? By no means! We are those who have died to sin; how can we live in it any longer? Or don't you know that all of us who were baptized into Christ Jesus were baptized into his death? We were therefore buried with him through baptism into death in order that, just as Christ was raised from the dead through the glory of the Father, we too may live a new life."

Romans 6:1- 4

"Having been buried with him in baptism, in which you were also raised with him through your faith in the working of God, who raised him from the dead."

Colossians 2:12

DRENCHED! (1)

What sort of people are buried? Spiritually, how does this make sense of what's happened to you?

> ✎

2. When to be Baptised

'Now an angel of the Lord said to Philip, "Go south to the road—the desert road—that goes down from Jerusalem to Gaza." So he started out, and on his way he met an Ethiopian eunuch, an important official in charge of all the treasury of the Kandake (which means "queen of the Ethiopians"). This man had gone to Jerusalem to worship, and on his way home was sitting in his chariot reading the Book of Isaiah the prophet. The Spirit told Philip, "Go to that chariot and stay near it." Then Philip ran up to the chariot and heard the man reading Isaiah the prophet. "Do you understand what you are reading?" Philip asked. "How can I," he said, "unless someone   explains it to me?" So he invited Philip to come up and sit with him. This is the passage of Scripture the

DRENCHED! (1)

eunuch was reading: "He was led like a sheep to the slaughter, and as a lamb before its shearer is silent, so he did not open his mouth. In his humiliation he was deprived of justice. Who can speak of his descendants? For his life was taken from the earth." The eunuch asked Philip, "Tell me, please, who is the prophet talking about, himself or someone else?" Then Philip began with that very passage of Scripture and told him the good news about Jesus. As they travelled along the road, they came to some water and the eunuch said, "Look, here is water. What can stand in the way of my being baptised?" And he gave orders to stop the chariot. Then both Philip and the eunuch went down into the water and Philip baptised him. When they came up out of the water, the Spirit of the Lord suddenly took Philip away, and the eunuch did not see him again, but went on his way rejoicing.'

Acts 8:26 – 39

"And now what are you waiting for? Get up, be baptized and wash your sins away, calling on his name"

Acts 22:16

Talk to your church leader about when you can be baptised

3. A Final Thought

Baptism is more than just a symbolic act. Something very powerful can happen spiritually as you act in obedience to the Lord. As you go into the water, trust that God is going to set you free from things in the past that have held you back from following Jesus. Miracles can, and do, happen at baptism!

A Prayer

Lord Jesus, just as you were baptised, help me to follow in your steps.

In your Name, Amen

DRENCHED! (2)

The Holy Spirit is the one who makes Jesus real in our experience. He also gives us the ability to grow in our faith. This session focuses on how the Holy Spirit wants to impact our lives once we have become Christians.

1. God wants to fill us as well as forgive us!

"In my former book, Theophilus, I wrote about all that Jesus began to do and to teach until the day he was taken up to heaven, after giving instructions through the Holy Spirit to the apostles he had chosen. After his suffering, he presented himself to them and gave many convincing proofs that he was alive. He appeared to them over a period of forty days and spoke about the kingdom of God. On one occasion, while he was eating with them, he gave them this command: "Do not leave Jerusalem, but wait for the gift my Father promised, which you have heard me speak about. For John baptized with water, but in a few days you will be baptized with the Holy Spirit."

Acts 1: 1 - 5

What was the 'gift my Father promised'?

How is this gift described in Acts 2:4?

Has this happened for you yet?

DRENCHED! (2)

2. How to be filled (baptised, drenched) with the Holy Spirit

'On the last and greatest day of the Festival, Jesus stood and said in a loud voice, "Let anyone who is thirsty come to me and drink. Whoever believes in me, as Scripture has said, rivers of living water will flow from within them." By this he meant the Spirit, whom those who believed in him were later to receive. Up to that time the Spirit had not been given, since Jesus had not yet been glorified.'

John 7: 37 – 39

Jesus says there are three steps to take:

- T_____

- C_____ to J_____

- D_____

In your own words, try and describe what these steps mean for you

DRENCHED! (2)

"So I say to you: Ask and it will be given to you; seek and you will find; knock and the door will be opened to you. For everyone who asks receives; those who seek find; and to those who knock, the door will be opened. "Which of you fathers, if your son asks for a fish, will give him a snake instead? Or if he asks for an egg, will give him a scorpion? If you then, though you are evil, know how to give good gifts to your children, how much more will your Father in heaven give the Holy Spirit to those who ask him!"

Luke 11: 9 – 13

What do we need to do (given that we have sorted out the above three steps) in order to receive the Holy Spirit fully?

---

3. Why is it important to be baptised with the Holy Spirit?

Read each passage and then answer in your own words:

Acts 1: 8

DRENCHED! (2)

Galatians 5: 22 – 23

1 Corinthians 12: 7 – 11

What's the link between the above passages and keeping the Great Command?

A Prayer

Lord Jesus, fill me, baptise me, flood me, drench me with your Holy Spirit. Let me receive from you so that I can give back to you. May your presence overflow from me and touch the lives of those around me.

In your Name, Amen

KNOWING GOD (1)

Being a follower of Jesus is all about having a friendship with God.
This friendship begins when we do three things:

• Turn away from our own way of living and turn to the Lord, confessing our selfishness, wrongdoing and rebellion against him.

• Put our trust in what Jesus did on the cross, dying to take the punishment for us so that we can be forgiven and brought back to God.

• Asking the living Lord Jesus to make his presence real in our lives through his Holy Spirit who comes to live in us, giving us a spiritual birth.

How do we get to know God better?

There are two main ways.

• Through learning more about him = the Bible (often called the Scriptures)

"All Scripture is God-breathed and is useful for teaching, rebuking, correcting and training in righteousness, so that all God's people may be thoroughly equipped for every good work."

2 Timothy 3:16-17

• Through conversation with him = Prayer

"But when you pray, go into your room, close the door and pray to your Father, who is unseen. Then your Father, who sees what is done in secret, will reward you. And when you pray, do not keep on babbling like pagans, for they think they will be heard because of their many words. Do not be like them, for your Father knows what you need before you ask him. This, then, is how you should pray: Our Father in heaven, hallowed be your name, your kingdom come, your

KNOWING GOD (1)

will be done, on earth as it is in heaven. Give us today our daily bread. And forgive us our debts, as we also have forgiven our debtors. And lead us not into temptation, but deliver us from the evil one.

Matthew 6:5 - 14

The Bible

It's a big book! In fact it's 66 books in one.

So where to start . . .

1. A Plan of Action

• Start by reading through the whole of Mark's Gospel. You can either do it in one sitting of a few hours, or twenty minutes a day for about a week. This will give you an overview of who Jesus is and the amazing things he said and did.

• Back to chapter one! Each day, try and read one small section (usually between 5 – 10 verses).

• Before you read, ask God to help you, teach you, speak to you.

• Read at normal speed

• Read it again slowly, thinking about it carefully

• Ask questions – why, when, who, what, how?

• Is there anything that speaks into your personal situation? Is there a promise? Is there direction? Is there something to adjust in your life?

• More than anything else, what does it show you about Jesus?

KNOWING GOD (1)

"You study the Scriptures diligently because you think that in them you possess eternal life. These are the very Scriptures that testify about me, yet you refuse to come to me to have life."

John 5: 39-40

2. Thank the Lord for what he has shown you and use it as a springboard into prayer.

3. What next?

• Get yourself a modern translation of the Bible and/or download a Bible app onto your phone or tablet.

• Get some advice on tools to help you understand and apply what you are reading.

KNOWING GOD (1)

A Prayer

Dear Lord,
Getting to know you will be a lifetime of discovery! Thank you for giving us the Bible so that we can find out who you are and what you do.
As I learn more, may it cause me to love you more and then may that love spill over to people around me.

In Jesus Name, Amen

KNOWING GOD (2)

Imagine a friendship where there was little if any conversation.
It couldn't exist!

Prayer is 'vertical conversation'!

1. How to Pray

Read Matthew 6:5 – 14

Talking with God can be the most natural thing in the world. The outline that Jesus gives in Matthew 6 is not meant to be repeated parrot-fashion. But it does give us an outline of the sort of things we should be talking to God about.

'Our Father in Heaven'

• Remind yourself who you're talking to.

• Thank him for making you one of his children.

'Hallowed be your name'

• Pray that he would be honoured - in your life, family, church, nation, the world.

• Be specific – think of particular situations where God needs to be honoured.

'Your kingdom come, your will be done....'

•Lord, where does your rule (kingdom) need to break in?

• Where is your will being ignored and I need to pray for change?

KNOWING GOD (2)

'Give us today our daily bread'

• Ask for what you need and for the needs of others.

'Forgive us our debts, as we also have forgiven our debtors'

• Is there anyone I need to forgive?

• Is there anything for which I need forgiveness?

'And lead us not into temptation, but deliver us from the evil one'

• Pray for God to strengthen you so you can resist temptation.

• Thank him for the reality of 1John 4:4 and 1Corinthians 10:13.

'Yours is the kingdom, the power and the glory forever. Amen'

• Finish with praise and worship, because he's in control and he's worth it!

2. Practising His Presence

"Where can I go from your Spirit? Where can I flee from your presence?
If I go up to the heavens, you are there; if I make my bed in the depths, you are
there. If I rise on the wings of the dawn, if I settle on the far side of the sea, even
there your hand will guide me, your right hand will hold me fast. If I say, "Surely
the darkness will hide me and the light become night around me," even the
darkness will not be dark to you; the night will shine like the day, for darkness is
as light to you."

Psalm 139:7 - 12

KNOWING GOD (2)

Learn to remember that the Lord is always with you! You don't have to be speaking to know his presence!

> **What practical thing could you do to learn to remember he's with you?**
>
> ✎

3. 'Arrow' Prayers

In the course of the day, you can send up lots of short requests or words of love to God. You don't even have to open your mouth!

> **Think about a regular part of your day/week when it would be very helpful to 'shoot a prayer up'.**
>
> ✎

KNOWING GOD (2)

It's two-way

God speaks to us in prayer, often to guide us, challenge us or comfort us. It can happen in a variety of ways:

• The 'gentle whisper' in our hearts (1 Kings 19:12)
• Through a sense of peace (Colossians 3:15)
• Lots of other ways!

Here are two ways of testing whether it's really God speaking to you:

• Does it fit in with the Great Command? (Love God/love others)
• Does it fit in with what the Bible teaches?

A Prayer

Father in heaven, many thanks for the privilege of being able to talk with you! You are the Creator, I'm just a creature. But still you care for me. Amazing!

Amen

GOD'S FAMILY

What is church?

- It's not a building, with or without a steeple

- It's not just what happens on Sundays

- It's not just for very old people, although they are very welcome!

In the New Testament, there are many different images used to describe the church. Here are just two!

1. Church is a Family

"For this reason I kneel before the Father, from whom every family in heaven and on earth derives its name".

Ephesians 3:14 - 15

God is our Father, so what are we to each other?

What words describe a good family?

GOD'S FAMILY

How many of these should apply to church?

✎

2. Church is the Body of Christ

"Just as a body, though one, has many parts, but all its many parts form one body, so it is with Christ. For we were all baptized by one Spirit so as to form one body - whether Jews or Gentiles, slave or free - and we were all given the one Spirit to drink. Even so the body is not made up of one part but of many. Now if the foot should say, "Because I am not a hand, I do not belong to the body," it would not for that reason cease to be part of the body. And if the ear should say, "Because I am not an eye, I do not belong to the body," it would not for that reason cease to be part of the body. If the whole body were an eye, where would the sense of hearing be? If the whole body were an ear, where would the sense of smell be? But in fact God has placed the parts in the body, every one of them, just as he wanted them to be. If they were all one part, where would the body be? As it is, there are many parts, but one body."

1 Corinthians 12:12- 20

GOD'S FAMILY

When Jesus was physically around 2000 years ago, what were the main things he did?

How should this influence what the church does in the 21st century?

GOD'S FAMILY

Have you thought about your contribution to the Body?

3. 'To Do' List

• Sunday church services are a place to enjoy celebrating God's goodness and to receive teaching, so go!

• Join a small midweek group for friendship and spiritual growth .

• Discover opportunities to use your gifts and abilities to help others.

• Be ready to introduce people to God's family.

A Prayer

Father, thank you for your family, the church. Thank you for a bunch of people who, though not perfect, love one another, love you and want to reach others with your love.
Help me to be a contributor in your body and not simply a consumer!
Lord Jesus, build your church strong and large!

In your Name, Amen

SHARING GOOD NEWS

Think about a time when you heard some good news. What was your natural desire?

✎

The word 'Gospel' means good news. We have some fantastic news to share with our friends, family, neighbours and work colleagues!

"Praise be to the God and Father of our Lord Jesus Christ, who has blessed us in the heavenly realms with every spiritual blessing in Christ. For he chose us in him before the creation of the world to be holy and blameless in his sight. In love he predestined us for adoption to sonship through Jesus Christ, in accordance with his pleasure and will - to the praise of his glorious grace, which he has freely given us in the One he loves. In him we have redemption through his blood, the forgiveness of sins, in accordance with the riches of God's grace that he lavished on us.

Ephesians 1:3 – 10

Read this passage slowly. How many things has God done for us/given us through Jesus?

✎

Thank him in prayer for what he's done/is doing for you!

SHARING GOOD NEWS

1. Why should we tell others the Gospel?

• Try and find a reason from each of these places

John 3:16

✎

Matthew 28:18 - 20

✎

---

2 Corinthians 5:10 - 11

✎

---

2 Corinthians 5:20

✎

SHARING GOOD NEWS

2. How should we tell others the Gospel?

"But in your hearts revere Christ as Lord. Always be prepared to give an answer to everyone who asks you to give the reason for the hope that you have. But do this with gentleness and respect."

1 Peter 3:15

What has to happen first if we are to be effective at sharing about Jesus?

How else do you think we can we be prepared?

What are the two key words here concerning our attitude when we speak?

SHARING GOOD NEWS

3. Who would you most like to share this Good News with?

Ask God to show you who in particular you should be praying for regularly. Try and keep it down to three individuals or couples.

Write their names here:-

_____

_____

_____

_____

As you begin to pray for these people, expect the Lord to give you opportunities to share your faith with them in a natural way.

A Prayer

Father God, thank you for all you have done for me through Jesus. There are so many people who have never heard about your love, forgiveness and power to transform. Help me, Lord, to share what I've experienced with those around me, especially the people named above.

In your Name, Amen

MONEY, MONEY, MONEY

"No one can serve two masters. Either you will hate the one and love the other, or you will be devoted to the one and despise the other. You cannot serve both God and money."

Matthew 6:24

"But godliness with contentment is great gain. For we brought nothing into the world, and we can take nothing out of it. But if we have food and clothing, we will be content with that. Those who want to get rich fall into temptation and a trap and into many foolish and harmful desires that plunge people into ruin and destruction. For the love of money is a root of all kinds of evil. Some people, eager for money, have wandered from the faith and pierced themselves with many griefs."

1 Timothy 6:6 – 10

Is money evil?

When does money become a problem for us?

MONEY, MONEY, MONEY

Money and material possessions consume the time, thinking and affections of so many of us in the 21st century. Money has become our god. Interestingly, Jesus spent a lot of time teaching on this subject, and it's picked up as well by the early church leaders.

Here are a few basic things to learn:

1. Learn to be generous

"Heal the sick, raise the dead, cleanse those who have leprosy, drive out demons. Freely you have received, freely give."

Matthew 1-:8

"For God so loved the world that he gave his one and only Son, that whoever believes in him shall not perish but have eternal life".

John 3:16

Why should we be generous?

2. Learn to have a good attitude

"Each of you should give what you have decided in your heart to give, not reluctantly or under compulsion, for God loves a cheerful giver."

2 Corinthians 9:7

"In everything I did, I showed you that by this kind of hard work we must help the weak, remembering the words the Lord Jesus himself said: 'It is more blessed to give than to receive.'"

Acts 20:35

MONEY, MONEY, MONEY

How do these attitudes differ from what many people would naturally feel?

3. Learn to be deliberate

"On the first day of every week, each one of you should set aside a sum of money in keeping with your income, saving it up, so that when I come no collections will have to be made."

1 Corinthians 16:2

What sort of principle is operating here?

What would happen to our giving if it wasn't planned?

MONEY, MONEY, MONEY

4. A Final Word

A famous Christian leader named Martin Luther commented that most people need two conversions: one of the heart and one of the wallet!

We can never 'outgive' God. Any sort of giving from us should be a response of gratitude for all the Lord has done for us.

There may be important things to talk through which may not have been dealt with here, such as the principle of tithing (Malachi 3: 6 – 10) or if you are dealing with debt.

A Prayer

Lord Jesus, you gave up everything for me when you came to earth and went to the cross. Everything I have is really yours. Please help me to love you and not to love money or possessions. Teach me to be a giver not a getter. Thank you that in giving, I will be mirroring who you are.

In your Name, Amen

ABOUT THE AUTHOR

Gary Gibbs is an ordained minister of the Elim Pentecostal Church.
Over the course of four decades, Gary has been involved in church planting,
an international travelling ministry and church leadership.

Today he is the director of REACH, the national evangelism and church
planting department of the Elim churches.
Gary is passionate about seeing people encounter Jesus and then going on
to become fully committed Christ followers.

He has been married to his best friend Sally for as long as he has been in
ministry and is the proud dad of three children and (at present) four grand-
children!